EMERSON FITTIPALDI

EMERSON FITTIPALDI
HEART OF A RACER

 KARL LUDVIGSEN

Foreword by Teddy Mayer

Haynes Publishing

To Sam with love

First published in November 2002

A catalogue record for this book is available from the British Library

ISBN 1 85960 837 X

Library of Congress control no. 2002107502

Haynes North America Inc., 861 Lawrence Drive, Newbury Park, California 91320, USA.

Published by Haynes Publishing, Sparkford, Yeovil, Somerset BA22 7JJ, UK.
Tel: 01963 442030 Fax: 01963 440001
Int.tel: +44 1963 442030 Int.fax: +44 1963 440001
E-mail: sales@haynes-manuals.co.uk
Website: www.haynes.co.uk

Typeset by Glad Stockdale, Sutton
Printed and bound in Britain by J.H. Haynes & Co. Ltd., Sparkford

Jacket illustrations
Front cover: Winning the Race of Champions at Brands Hatch at the start of the 1972 season proves an excellent omen for Fittipaldi, who goes on to win his first World Championship that season. Britain's Fleet Street dubs him the 'Black Prince' in his black and gold Lotus 72. (Max Le Grand from Ludvigsen Library)

Back cover: In his 1990 CART season Emerson proudly carries the number 1 on his Penske PC19 as reigning drivers' champion. He joins the Penske team that year after a determined 1989 in which he attacks the series with renewed vigour and records five victories on his way to the championship. (Bob Tronolone)

Frontispiece
From day one, an open and engaging smile is one of Emerson Fittipaldi's greatest assets, both as a racing driver and as a global personality. Behind it, however, fizzes a shrewd racing brain of the first magnitude.

Contents

Introduction

Emerson owes me a dinner. At least that's what I remind him whenever we meet, because in my days as a Ford executive I organised a dinner for him at London's Carlton Tower Hotel when he retired as a Grand Prix driver. And then he unretired! The nerve of the guy! But as this book will make clear, there was no arguing with the merit of his decision.

We originally met at the auto show in Sao Paulo in 1968, when I had my first look at auto racing Brazilian-style – quite an eye-opener. Heavy restrictions on imports meant that enthusiastic improvisation was the order of the day, and the Fittipaldi brothers were in the vanguard. I kept up with Emerson's burgeoning career through the Brazilian magazine *Quatro Rodas* for which we both wrote, with the result that I was probably one of the scant handful of people at Watkins Glen in 1970 who had any inkling of the identity of the surprise winner of the US Grand Prix.

The day after the Glen race I had the honour of hosting dinner for Emerson and Maria Helena at Le Chanteclair in New York, then the watering hole for racing fans owned by René and Maurice Dreyfus. René, of course, had raced successfully for Maserati, Bugatti and the Scuderia Ferrari. We also arranged to drive the Fittipaldis to Kennedy Airport for their trip home, and on the way Emerson regaled me with the tale of the twin-engined Beetle he and his brother built and raced. The saga was so hilarious it was all I could do to keep my BMW on the Van Wyck Expressway, we were laughing so hard.

Future visits to Brazil, courtesy of the auto show's management, gave me more chances to interview Emerson and to enjoy his family's warm hospitality at Morumbi and Guarujá. Although his daughter Juliana won't remember it, I was the first man to bring her flowers! Later my son Miles and I paid a call at the European Fittipaldi base near Lausanne.

In October 1973 we had a surprise reunion when we were both at Porsche's Weissach development centre near Stuttgart. I was there to research my book on Porsche and he was there to try both the Carrera that would be used in the International Race of Champions or 'IROC' series and a turbocharged 917 Can-Am test car. 'He was only so-so in the Carrera,' said Porsche chief Ernst Fuhrmann afterwards, 'but he was *outstanding* in the 917 turbo.'

Prompted by his fascination with this amazing car, Fittipaldi had a few outings in a turbocharged Porsche

917 in the Interserie, Germany's Can-Am counterpart. This was one of his rare departures from single-seater competition. In his complete and utter dedication to open-wheeled *monoposto* racers Emerson was unusual in his era, indeed exceptional. Le Mans and the Can-Am series were not on his agenda, making him the first of the modern breed of dedicated Grand Prix and CART racers. 'You have to drive long-distance races bearing in mind that the engine needs saving as it has to last until the end,' Emerson explained. 'In the case of single-seaters it's a sprint to the finish. That's what I like most.'

On one of his rare sports-racing outings Fittipaldi suffered a smash that was by far his worst until his career-ending impact of 1996. During practice for the 1971 1000 kilometres of Buenos Aires he crashed his Type 33 Alfa Romeo into the guard rails at high speed when a tyre deflated, punctured by a wire from the steel brushes that were used to sweep the course clean! Miraculously he was unhurt. Emerson hopped into a Porsche 917, co-driving with Carlos Reutemann, but retired with oil on its clutch 'after a good run'.

His other enclosed-car races were in the IROC series, in each of which a dozen selected champion racers did battle in identical cars on both road circuits and ovals. Fittipaldi competed five times, from the inaugural 1974 IROC to the 1990 races – a remarkable span. For the very first race at Riverside in Porsche Carreras he qualified on pole, but had to start last after missing the drivers' meeting – doubtless having overslept. He finished third in two Riverside races and was ranked seventh overall. Switching to Chevrolet Camaros, Emerson was fifth overall in the '75 IROC, winning the second race at Riverside.

In the 1976 series he was eighth overall, and the same again in 1979. When the IROC races were reborn in 1984 – his first season back at the wheel – Fittipaldi was nominated. That was his worst-ever year with a next-to-last ranking. He last drove the IROC cars in 1990 when Dodge Daytonas were used. Finishing sixth overall for his next-to-best placing, he collected his biggest-ever IROC cheque of $38,000.

When I saw Emerson that October of 1973 at Porsche, he told me that his brother Wilson Jr. – then driving in Formula 1 for Brabham – would leave the tracks for a year and return in 1975. I replied, 'Clearly you'll have your own car by then.' 'You are too quick!' Fittipaldi rejoined with a grin. At a dinner in New York a year later he showed me pictures of the first Grand Prix Fittipaldi under construction, and in November, 1974 I watched some of its early tests at Interlagos.

I believe that this book will put that ambitious project – and Emerson's role in it – in its proper perspective for the first time. If that is so it will be thanks to the help of Richard Divila and Jo Ramirez, who generously took time to explain their Fittipaldi years to me. I owe very special thanks to Teddy Mayer, both for his illuminating comments on Emerson Fittipaldi's career and for his foreword to this book. Teddy occupies a unique position as a protagonist in Emerson's two championship lives in Formula 1 and CART racing.

No one writing about Emerson can do so without consulting Elizabeth Hayward's book about his early career, *Flying on the Ground*, and Gordon Kirby's later work, *Emerson Fittipaldi*. All quotes from these books are referenced in the text, as are those from other contemporary sources. The annotated bibliography provides additional information about research sources. All responsibility for errors of fact or interpretation lies with the author.

A word is needed as well about the talented photographers whose images illuminate this book. From the Ludvigsen Library we display predominantly the work of Max Le Grand, Ove Nielsen and (less talented) yours truly, while Bob Tronolone has portrayed Fittipaldi's Stateside career with his usual skill.

I need no excuse for beginning this book with a chapter about Emerson's amazing career in the Indianapolis 500-mile race. It will, I think, put to rest for once and for all the notion that his skill and drive deteriorated along with the performance of his Copersucars in the late 1970s. Fittipaldi's is an unmatched story of high ambition and focused determination, married in an engaging and eternally youthful personality.

Karl Ludvigsen
Hawkedon, Suffolk
2002

Foreword

by Teddy Mayer

McLaren Team Principal 1964–1982 and Penske Racing Director 1987–2001

I have great pleasure in writing this Foreword to Karl Ludvigsen's book about Emerson Fittipaldi. I worked with Emerson in both Formula 1 and Indycar racing and value greatly not only his competence as a driver but also his personal friendship.

When Emerson joined McLaren for the 1974 Formula 1 season he brought with him the Marlboro sponsorship, an affiliation which continued for him on and off for the next 20 years. Relationships were, and are, important to Emerson. As a firm believer in teamwork, he works hard to surround himself with competent people to help him achieve his objectives. This characteristic helped Fittipaldi win two Formula 1 World Championships when not yet 28 and, unbelievable as it may seem, 21 years later an Indycar race when almost 49. In the outstanding success of his two consecutive careers Emerson is unmatched by any other driver.

Would-be young racers could do much worse than copy Emerson's technique. Emerson was generally steady and reliable rather than blindingly quick, but when required he could definitely get with the program. His analytical approach to car set-up and meticulous pre-race planning were a formidable combination which, added to his very

real driving skills, made him one of the most successful drivers of all time – especially on the big occasions when the pressure was extreme.

However, I wouldn't suggest to prospective drivers that they emulate Emerson's style of timekeeping. There is on-time, late, Brazilian time and 'Emerson time'. Emerson was never just late. He could more or less manage the official schedule of a race weekend, but he tended to arrive at sponsor functions just when most of the guests were about to leave and he often showed up for morning meetings in the early afternoon.

Emerson just planned his life in a certain way and got around to fulfilling other obligations when it suited him. We learned to make allowances for this, but it drove the punctilious Kiwis on the McLaren team crazy. If his intense dedication to his professional duties as a driver had been carried over to his off-track activities, he would indeed have been the perfect racing driver.

Patience is an attribute which top-flight racing drivers must have. More than in any other sport, a driver's results are often affected by mechanical problems or other circumstances entirely outside his control. This applies especially to the hard slog of testing, where Emerson was

In a conversation with a Goodyear tyre engineer (out of shot), Emerson takes the lead while McLaren's Teddy Mayer listens. At an appropriate point Teddy joins in, to Fittipaldi's amusement. In both the 1970s and the 1990s the two make a formidable team.

especially adept. The Latin temperament is not normally credited with having patience, but Emerson's professional career was characterised by a remarkably cool and calculating approach. In two seasons at McLaren, he only spun once and I don't remember one instance of damage to his car. This is a singular statistic for a driver operating at the sport's cutting edge.

There is no doubt that his 1974 Grand Prix World Championship was down to his patience. The McLaren M23 did not feel right to Emerson for the first half of the season and he pushed hard for modifications. Finally at Silverstone we tested revised suspension geometry front and rear in readiness for the upcoming British Grand Prix at Brands Hatch. Afterward Emerson told me, 'Teddy, with this car now I can fight for the World Championship.' And indeed he did, prevailing in a tremendously competitive season.

In the 1994 Indianapolis 500-mile race that forms the structure of Karl's first chapter Emerson led most of the

way. With only 20-odd laps to go he was almost a lap in front of his second-place team-mate, Al Unser Jnr. Aware that he would have to make another pit stop, he was frantic to know whether Al would also have to stop again. His crew were unsure and – as Karl describes – did not immediately answer so Emerson took a chance, passed Al going into Turn Four and crashed as a result. It was the only time I ever saw him make a serious mistake in a race.

After that incident – again belying the stereotype of the tempestuous Latin – there were no recriminations whatsoever. Nor were there in 1995 when we at Penske failed to get Emerson into the 500-mile race which he had won twice before. Instead, he concluded that fate had decreed that he should not be in the 33-car field that year, and if indeed he's still around because he avoided a fatal crash by not racing at Indy in '95, I should add clairvoyance to my inventory of Fittipaldi attributes. Knowing Emerson as I do, it wouldn't surprise me.

CHAPTER 1

The Indy 4,462

In 1994 Emerson Fittipaldi already had two Indianapolis 500-mile wins under his belt. This assured him a place in Indy's pantheon alongside such immortals as Tommy Milton, Bill Vukovich and Rodger Ward. With a third win, however, he would match the achievements of Wilbur Shaw, Mauri Rose, Lou Meyer and Bobby Unser – men whose skills and artistry are writ large in the history of one of the world's greatest motor races.

For Emerson many omens were excellent in 1994. Every person entering the gates of the famed 2½-mile Speedway carried his picture with them – on their ticket, where he was portrayed as the previous year's winner. With Paul Tracy and Al Unser Jnr. he was driving the year's killer car, the Penske PC23 powered by a new Mercedes-Benz V-8 engine with pushrod-operated overhead valves that drove a cart and many horses through

Atop the Pontiac pace car, Emerson Fittipaldi prepares for a celebratory lap of the Indianapolis Motor Speedway after his first 500-mile victory there in 1989. Peering between him and wife Teresa is 'Pat' Patrick, his car owner and the man who brought Emerson back to top-line racing in the CART series.

the Indy rulebook, giving it an advantage over its rivals of more than 150 horsepower.

Throughout May Fittipaldi was consistently the fastest driver on the track. His was the month's fastest lap, a sizzling 230.438mph. He qualified on the outside of the front row at an average of 227.303mph for his four laps. In the race he made his first fuel stop after 23 laps and moved into the lead ahead of team-mate Unser. He headed the field through the 100-lap mid-race point and on his 121st lap, seven miles before his fourth pit stop, Fittipaldi set the event's fastest lap at 220.680mph – the only driver to top 220 during the 500 miles.

Not all of May's omens had been positive, however. On the first day of the month the man who was Emerson's successor as Brazil's auto-racing idol, Ayrton Senna, was killed at Imola. 'Everybody, even the most simple people, were feeling what happened to Ayrton,' Fittipaldi said of his countrymen, 'and the whole country stopped. It was incredible.' He joined Jackie Stewart, Gerhard Berger, Alain Prost and other racing notables at Senna's funeral in Brazil on May 5th.

Emerson was too professional to let thoughts of the death of his brilliant protégé cloud his concentration as he led the field at Indy in 1994. But tucked in a tiny corner of his grey matter was a recollection of his first visit to the Speedway 20 years earlier. As a youngster he'd been attracted to oil-additive Bardahl – an early personal sponsor – by the glamour of its association with Indianapolis. By 1974 he'd joined a team – McLaren – that was active in Indycar racing as well as Formula 1. Indeed it was more than active; McLaren's turbo-Offy-powered M16 won the Indy 500 in 1974 with Johnny Rutherford at the wheel. After a win at Watkins Glen in October that sealed his second World Championship that year, Emerson Fittipaldi travelled to Indianapolis to try Rutherford's papaya-orange car during the one-hour lunch breaks in Goodyear's tyre tests.

'It is a unique place in the world,' he said, 'very special, Indianapolis.' He found out just how special when he and Eoin Young first arrived at the gates of the hallowed track. They 'wished the aged guard good morning,' wrote Young, 'and announced our intention of joining the McLaren tyre-test crew inside the track. The guard never uttered a word but regarded us with supreme disinterest and then spat what I hope was a wad of tobacco some six feet in the direction we had planned to travel. Emerson thought that was just about the funniest thing he'd seen all morning but I felt that it was the ideal introduction for the new World Champion to the site of the Greatest Spectacle in Motor Racing!'

Emerson drove the M16 during two consecutive lunch hours. In the first he settled in with 16 laps, the quickest of which was 161mph – crawling by Indy standards. On his second day, however, he turned 40 laps and reached a speed of 183mph. This would have qualified him in the fifth of the 11 rows of that year's starting field. He had taken to the track with remarkable speed and ease. Fully occupied as he was at the time with his Grand Prix career, however, Fittipaldi gave no thought to jumping to Indycars.

Tucked in another tiny crevice of the Fittipaldi brain, during that dominant drive in 1994, was his recollection that he'd first raced at the Speedway ten years earlier – and ten years after he'd tried Johnny Rutherford's McLaren. Nineteen eighty-four was his first season back in racing after a three-year hiatus. On the fourth day of practice he breezed through the demeaning 'rookie' test

that every newcomer to the track must endure. Emerson's Indy race début was inauspicious. After sitting in his new March-Cosworth only the day before qualifying, he put it in the field – not everyone does – at just over 200mph but his car only lasted 37 laps before retiring with a shortage of oil pressure.

Emerson's 1984 form in CART racing was good enough to attract the attention of Uell E 'call me Pat' Patrick, a wealthy southern oilman who had been an Indycar team owner or partner since 1970. With Patrick's equipment Emerson qualified an excellent fifth in 1985 and managed to lead 11 laps before being snagged just 30 miles from the finish by fuel-line problems. He was proving a more-than-useful driver at the rectangular Speedway with its four challenging corners.

In 1986 Emerson's Patrick March-Cosworth appeared in a livery that was familiar from his spell with the McLaren Formula 1 team in 1974–75. It was the striking red and white motif of Marlboro. He kept it among the top speedsters during practice with 214-mph laps and vowed to set it up so he could qualify by running flat out. This worked well for his first two laps, which he turned at 213-plus, but a leak from one tyre forced him to back off for a four-lap average of 210.237. Slower by one mile per hour than his previous year's speed, this put him in the middle of the fourth row.

The 1986 start was delayed twice, once by almost a week on account of rain and again on race day when a car spun into the barriers on the parade lap. Fittipaldi kept his mount among the top half-dozen for most of the running. He led the 48th lap and was second at 80 laps. A miss from one cylinder, however, dropped him to seventh late in the race where he finished, a lap behind the winner. Prize money of $104,563 was some compensation for his efforts and those of the Patrick crew.

By now Emerson was applying to Indy the chassis-balancing skills that had brought him two Formula 1 World Championships. 'It's very high-precision work, very difficult,' he told Gordon Kirby. 'You must go through every detail, every tiny combination. The differences are very fine, very precise, and you have to feel these differences. It's much more sensitive than people realise. It's really the finest tuning you can do to any racing car in the world because the cornering speeds are so fast. At

Indianapolis we were approaching Turn 1 at 240mph and when you are behind two or three other cars at that speed, the turbulence is so great. Setting up a car to achieve the maximum speed at Indianapolis is the finest final tuning you can do to any racing car anywhere in the world. The more I learn, the more I love it. It's great!'

Fittipaldi's enthusiasm for the fine art of racing at Indianapolis was sorely tested in 1987. Still with Patrick and Marlboro, he was now powered by Chevrolet's new Indy engine built by Britain's Ilmor Engineering. With practice times in the 211 bracket he was looking forward to qualifying, but the clocks said 205.584mph. "I'm very disappointed,' said the Brazilian. 'It's very difficult to qualify here. There are so many people watching.'

He wished they weren't watching on 'carburetion day,' the last practice day before the race. Trying a different set of tyres because 'the car was feeling a little strange,' he spun into the Turn 3 wall and damaged the March too badly to be repaired for the race. He was allowed to shift to a backup March but was sent to the very tail end of the 33-car starting field. Emerson worked steadily forward and was running eighth when his Chevy V-8 failed him on the 131st lap.

Pat Patrick fine-tuned his team for the 1988 season. He cut back to a single Marlboro-backed car for Fittipaldi and brought Briton Morris 'Mo' Nunn on board to engineer it. With both a Lola and a March available, the Brazilian qualified the latter at 212.564mph with a best lap faster than 213. Well poised to start from the middle of the third row, Emerson was lucky to miss a first-lap tangle among several drivers near him in the starting field.

Unhappy with the handling, he asked Nunn for a wing adjustment at his first pit stop. Better balance helped him climb through the field to sixth by mid-race. A six-second stop for a splash of fuel on lap 168 helped Fittipaldi get back on the leader's lap. Any chance for a final challenge to 1988 winner Rick Mears was lost when the yellow flag came out for the 14th time for the final laps. Emerson finished second, the only other racer on the same lap as Mears and just seven seconds behind the Penske-team driver. Although his average for the yellow-marred race was a sluggish 144.726mph, his $353,103 for second place was awarded just the same.

For the 1989 race Pat Patrick and his partner Chip Ganassi put new Penske-built chassis under Emerson and his Chevy engine. The result was dramatic. On Indy's second practice day he was the first driver to break the 220mph barrier with a lap at 221.347. 'It was the first day we've run on a high-speed oval,' he explained, 'and I was getting used to the car.' He credited both the Speedway's new surface and better tyres for the uptick in speed. Before qualifying his best lap was a stunning 225.000mph precisely.

Emerson qualified at 222.329mph to sit on the front row for the first time. 'Today is the first day I feel like an Indycar driver,' he said afterward. 'It's a big achievement for my career. The car was balanced, but I lost about half an inch of boost, which cost us some speed.' He started from the outside of the front row, which he shared with the Penske team's Rick Mears and Al Unser.

'Indycar driver' Fittipaldi jumped into an immediate lead and was almost two seconds ahead after the first lap, which he turned at 209.2mph, *seven miles per hour* faster than the previous first-lap record. The early laps saw a duel of the legends, Mario Andretti chasing Emerson hard. Although his son Michael was the first to record a race lap of better than 220mph, and would lead for 35 laps, Fittipaldi left the record at an awesome 222.469mph while dominating the early laps.

Emerson was leading Al Unser Jnr. by just two seconds when both entered the crucial final ten laps. Back-markers played a crucial role as the pair battled for the lead. 'Little Al' closed relentlessly. 'It was like a nightmare when I saw Al Junior coming,' Fittipaldi told Gordon Kirby. 'It was like you dream you were running and you're stuck in the same place. When he was right behind me I looked in my mirror and I could see he was much faster than me on the straight. I said to myself, "There's no way I can stop him." And he did overtake me quite easily.'

With four laps to go Unser was leading. The crowd was on its feet and even the corner workers were urging on their favourites in one of the most dramatic *mano a mano* duels the venerable Speedway had seen. On-car cameras put television viewers in the cockpits of two cars, only one of which could win the race. Little Al tried to shake off the Brazilian, but a lap later he was still there

– and a lap after that. As they started the penultimate lap Emerson prepared his challenge: 'It was like someone pushed me from behind and said, "Emerson, come on. Go for it. You can still do it."'

Going into Turn 3 Fittipaldi was just below Unser and half a length behind, closing on two other cars. The Marlboro Penske drifted up and the two just touched – a puff of smoke from their tyres – and both were swerving, Emerson's under control but Unser's spinning into the wall and sliding down to the infield. Fittipaldi completed his final lap under the yellow and behind the pace car – in first place. 'It was a classic race,' he said. 'I think it is one race that nobody will ever repeat, one that never will happen in motor racing again. It was so close going through Turn 3. I was on the inside, he was on the outside, and we knew each other were not going to back off. That was a very dramatic moment for me. I would have been very frustrated not to have won that race.' His winning average was 167.581mph.

'In the winner's circle the feelings were just incredible,' Emerson recalled. Shoulders heaving with emotion, it was all he could do to keep his composure. 'I was 42 years old, and it was unbelievable I could win Indianapolis. That was one of the most emotional moments of my whole life. After so many years of disappointment and hard work, it was the special bonus. The dream come true. There's no doubt it was the most important single win of my career. I got more coverage for winning that race than I did winning my second World Championship.' Bolstered by the $71,100 he earned by leading 158 laps, Fittipaldi's cheque for his victory was $1,001,604, the first million-dollar pay day in Indy history.

Snapped up for the 1990 season by the powerful Penske team, Emerson soon showed that he was ready for his second win. His spectacular practice speeds culminated in a 227mph lap, the Speedway's first ever, capped by 228mph on the morning before qualifying. The first to attempt a four-lap run, Fittipaldi was also the fastest, seizing his first Indy pole with a record average of 225.301mph. All four of his laps were the first ever turned in qualifying in less than 40 seconds. 'The car was beautiful,' said Fittipaldi. 'It was just getting quicker and quicker.'

'The car was very good,' recalled Teddy Mayer, who was engineering Emerson's car. 'He was very happy with the chassis. We were really hooked up. He was comfortable running those speeds, so much so that he started to blister tyres that nobody else even began to blister. We had scrubbed all our sets of tyres once and I wanted to double-scrub them all.' Giving them an extra scrubbing would increase their resistance to heat and reduce the blistering that murdered tyres. 'Goodyear said no,' Teddy continued. 'They didn't want us to do that.'

Fittipaldi maintained his record-breaking form in the race proper. Diving under team-mate Mears, he seized the first-lap lead. He set records for the first 10 and 20 laps at 211.947 and 209.587mph respectively that still stand at this writing. The Brazilian dominated the running, turning his 91st lap at a record 222.574mph before pitting. At 110 and 130 laps he set new record speeds – still standing – of 177.039 and 180.624mph. 'Emerson was leading at about three-quarter distance,' said Teddy Mayer. 'He was miles – three-quarters of a lap – ahead when he ran into some blisters on a set of tyres. And that cost him an extra stop and the race. I could have killed Goodyear!' The extra pit stop dropped him to third at the finish of a race he seemed odds-on to win.

Tyre blistering was on Emerson's mind as he charged toward victory in the 1994 race. Roger Penske's team, the most respected in Indycar racing, had learned from the 1990 fiasco. Lessons had been learned as well from the 1991 and '92 races, neither of which saw a Fittipaldi greet the final flag. In 1991 Indy qualifying turned sour when Roger Penske aborted his four-lap run, which would have averaged better than 222mph, to make a later try – only to have an Indiana thunderstorm stop play. 'Sometimes racing works against you and sometimes it works in your favour,' said Emerson. 'Today it went against me.' On the following day he was in the race – on the outside of the fifth row – with a 223.064mph average.

Charging through the 1991 field, Fittipaldi took the lead on the 109th lap. Battling with Bobby Rahal, team-mate Rick Mears and Michael Andretti, he was leading at the 150-lap mark and again on lap 167, when he made his final stop for fuel and tyres. However, when he restarted, the Penske was visibly struggling. He pitted again on the 171st lap to retire with transmission failure. Emerson had to settle for 11th place.

In 1992 Fittipaldi put his Penske-Chevy in the middle of the fourth row with a qualifying average of 223.607mph. 'The car handled beautifully,' he said. 'I just needed a little more power. We should be looking good for the race.' At 60 laps Emerson's forecast was holding up; he was running a comfortable third. He was still there at 70 laps but on lap 76, while two other rivals were crashing, he too spun and hit the wall between Turns 1 and 2. Fortunately escaping serious injury, he was ranked 24th among 1992's starters.

In 1993 Emerson and the other Speedway drivers were learning to cope with a new feature of the track, laterally grooved 'rumble strips' below the white lines that defined the lower periphery of the turns. In qualifying Fittipaldi put a spare Penske PC22 into the field at 220.150mph. Starting ninth, Emerson gradually made up ground on the leaders, helped by a copybook half-dozen pit stops that took a total of 85 seconds. His late-race rivals were Arie Luyendyk, the 1990 Indy winner, and Britain's Nigel Mansell, making his maiden foray into Indycar racing.

On lap 186 – 35 miles from the finish – Fittipaldi seized the lead. He daunted his rivals with a series of quick laps, his 198th the fastest of the race at 214.807mph. The crowd jumped to its feet to see a real battle for victory with the first eight cars in the race covered by eight seconds. Red-gloved right fist brandished high, Emerson crossed the finish line with a 2.9-second advantage over Luyendyk and 4.2 seconds ahead of Mansell in third. Emerson had won his second Indianapolis 500-mile race and the ninth such success for Roger Penske's team.

'We didn't have to do anything to the car,' the Brazilian told Gordon Kirby. 'The only change we made in the whole race was when I moved the anti-roll bar one notch. That was all we did.' Not to be sneezed at, as well, was a victory cheque for $1,155,300. 'It's like a bonus for me,' said Fittipaldi, adding that it was 'the best race of my life, and the most important victory in my career at this stage. I have worked very hard on my physical condition and my diet. I am very motivated, and I think I can drive a racing car better than when I was twenty-five.'

In the winner's circle, however, Emerson made a major boo-boo. Since the years before World War II an Indy tradition had been a victory swig from a bottle of milk. Here was an all-American gesture to the dairy farmers of the Midwest, the nation's breadbasket. Instead Fittipaldi, owner of vast orange groves and a major supplier of juice concentrate, drank from a bottle of orange juice. Shock! Horror! Indy tradition not respected! He reached for the milk a moment later, but the damage had been done. Fans who had idolised the genial Brazilian suddenly had their doubts about him.

Now, in the 1994 race, Fittipaldi completed his pit-stop complement. On lap 133 he took on a splash of fuel while his crew cleared track debris from his radiator ducts. A 17-second stop on lap 164 was his longest for both tyres and fuel. Behind him, 30 seconds in arrears, was his team-mate 'Little Al' Unser in an identical Penske-Mercedes. Gaining ground on Al, Emerson passed him on lap 181 to be a full lap – 2½ miles – in the lead. Fittipaldi's last 100 miles were covered at 205.5mph, including a pit stop. He seemed an unstoppable force.

Only one thing nagged at the Brazilian. Unser had stopped four laps later than he. If there were no yellow lights, Emerson would have to make a final quick stop for more fuel. But would Little Al? 'That's the only time I've ever heard Emerson in a panic,' said Penske man Teddy Mayer, who was listening in on the radio link between Fittipaldi and his engineer Chuck Sprague. Emerson kept asking whether Little Al would have to make another stop. 'Clearly he would have to,' said Mayer, 'but Chuck Sprague kept asking Roger Penske and Roger wouldn't tell Chuck. Instead of Chuck saying, "Don't worry about it," to Emerson he kept saying, "I'm trying to find out. I'll find out."'

This wasn't going well, thought Mayer: 'In fact the answers just kept obviously irritating Emerson. I was listening in and I thought, Oh Christ, I can't say anything. it's absolutely *verboten*. It was so obvious that Al had to stop, I don't know why Chuck didn't just say, "Don't worry about it." But he didn't. And Emerson kept getting more and more agitated.' Unser had unlapped himself, which would have allowed him to catch Fittipaldi if a yellow flag were thrown. Emerson charged after his red-and-white team-mate, his tyres howling over the track's new rumble strips.

As the two cars careered into the final turn of the 185th lap Fittipaldi went low, preparing to pass Unser. 'Going into turn four,' he said, 'I tried to go a little lower than Junior and hit the apron. I hit the corrugation. I was about half a foot too low.' The tail darted out and – defying its driver's efforts to reassert control – crashed into the wall, the Penske sliding along the retaining wall at diminishing speed. 'I nearly corrected it,' said Emerson, 'but it was too late. It was a disaster! I had everything under control. The car was flying. We should have been one–two. I am very disappointed.'

Saved by a yellow light that let him slough off speed and fuel consumption, Unser cruised to victory while Fittipaldi was taken to the medical centre for a checkup. Still ringing in his ears were the cheers that erupted from the crowd when his car ground to a halt. They'd not forgotten Emerson's initial rejection of the milk the year before. They celebrated the downfall of the orange-juice drinker! From first place Fittipaldi plummeted to a lowly 17th.

If Indy 1994 seemed a bad dream to Emerson Fittipaldi, then 1995 became a nightmare. Penske's cars seemed incapable of the speed needed to qualify for the 500-mile race. Frequent rain delays hampered efforts to balance them properly. With a borrowed Lola, however, Emerson ran promising 227mph laps. 'I did a quick survey,' said Teddy Mayer, 'and it was very obvious that there was absolutely no way that if you ran 225 you wouldn't qualify. So I left that message with Emerson saying, "Here's what you've got to do. This is the speed you've got to run, and you know you can run it." I hoped that the message was going to get to Roger Penske – but it didn't or Roger panicked, one of the two.'

On the next-to-last qualifying day Fittipaldi ran his first three laps at better than a 225mph average but Penske signalled a 'wave-off' – a non-attempt – before the final lap was completed. 'In effect he was qualified,' said Mayer. 'His time would have put him about 30th – or 29th – and Roger waved him off.' Reportedly, the frustrated Brazilian unleashed a vituperative volley over the intercom that seared the ears of his colleagues. His attempt the following day was slower, and when another racer posted a faster time Emerson was knocked out of the 33-car field.

'The experience of motor racing is they can be wonderful and they can be a disaster,' he said. 'It was an incredible feeling not being able to qualify.' This maddening appearance at Indianapolis was his last. A Fittipaldi was in the field, however. His nephew Christian qualified for the first time. In the race he placed second and was elected Rookie of the Year.

As a two-time winner Emerson could have only good memories of his eleven 500-mile races. He left behind some marks for others to shoot at. Of his eleven races he led seven. His $227,250 placed him first among all Indy competitors in lap-prize winnings. Among the all-time lap leaders he is headed only by Al Unser, Ralph de Palma, Mario Andretti, A. J. Foyt and Wilbur Shaw. His career earnings at Indy of $4,042,767 were exceeded by only three drivers. In all, Emerson Fittipaldi covered 4,462 racing miles at the Indianapolis Motor Speedway. Not bad for a retread from the effete world of Grand Prix racing.

Captured behind the wheel of his Penske-Chevrolet at the Indianapolis 500-mile race in 1991, Emerson Fittipaldi is by then a proven threat on all CART circuits and an awesome and feared competitor at the legendary Indiana oval.

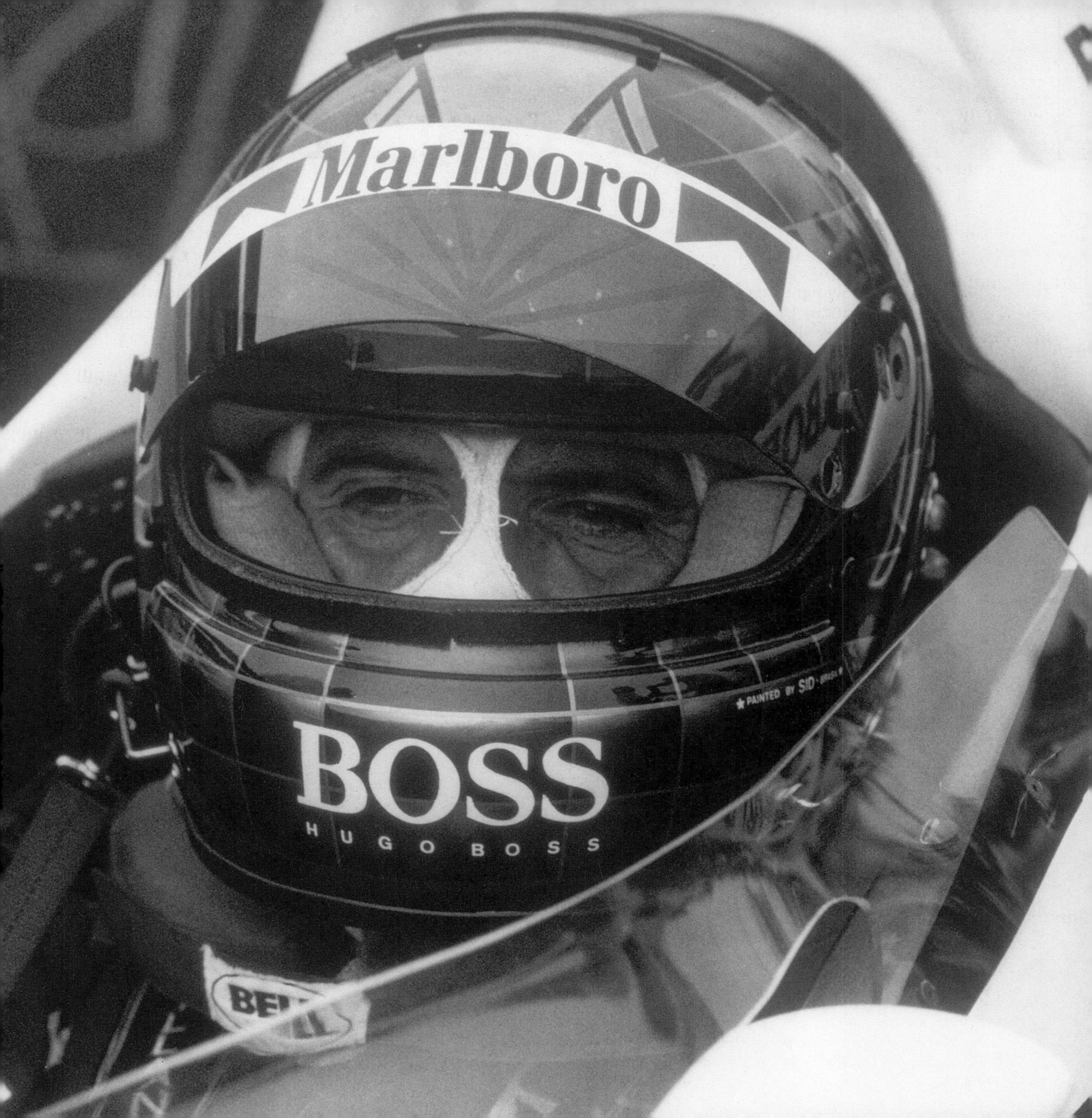
Marlboro
PAINTED BY SID
BOSS
HUGO BOSS

Emerson is seen at Indianapolis in 1984, 1985 and 1987 (top to bottom), the first two years in Cosworth-powered Marches and the last in a new March 87C with its still-fragile Chevrolet engine. His 1984 entry includes the number 7 he considers lucky and is coloured the same vivid fuchsia as his driving suit (right). In 1993 Fittipaldi is pictured by Bob Tronolone en route to his second Indianapolis victory in a Penske-Chevrolet (overleaf).

Emerson Fittipaldi easily earns his inclusion in a gathering of great Indianapolis drivers and winners. From left to right they are Johnny Rutherford, Emerson, A.J. Foyt, Al Unser, Bobby Rahal, Michael Andretti (only non-winner present), Mario Andretti, Al Unser Jnr. and Bobby Unser. Behind them is the famous Borg-Warner trophy on which all save Michael appear.

CHAPTER 2

The Mouse Who Roared

It's an exaggeration – albeit not excessive – to say that Brazilians could live on what falls from the trees. Their fabulously rich land was blessed by nature, from its Amazonian jungles to broad central plains and fruitful orchards of the south. Nature's only oversight was her failure to bless Brazil with oil. In the fuel-crisis years the fecundity of its agriculture easily allowed Brazil to close its 'gasoline gap' with alcohol from farm crops. Such is their land's natural prodigality that Brazil's citizens could be excused if they were a lazy, laid-back lot. Impressively, they are anything but.

Emerson himself portrayed the Brazilian character to Elizabeth Hayward: 'Sometimes in Brazil you have a man whose business is finished, he owes a lot of money, and really he is in a lot of trouble. But he is still smiling, and he'll say: "Oh, I'm going to work very hard and some day I will pay back all that I owe." But he can't be sad at

the time. He does not go out and shoot himself. We work very seriously and very hard in Brazil, but much more relaxed. The attitude is that if the problem is too difficult, okay, we'll try again tomorrow.'

Brazil's economy is a stimulating synthesis of North American products and concepts with native drive and ingenuity. If you are alert to global trends and well connected abroad, you can carve a profitable business niche in a nation whose wealthiest consumers are concentrated in and between the great coastal cities of Sao Paulo and Rio de Janeiro. Sprawling Sao Paulo alone, Brazil's industrial hub and capital of Sao Paulo State, has the capacity to spawn and support profitable enterprises. Here it was that the Fittipaldi brothers established bustling businesses in the fields that obsessed them: cars and racing.

Although not paved with gold, the dusty streets of Sao Paulo drew immigrants who wanted to try their luck in the New World. Among them was Emerson's paternal grandfather, who hailed from the small province of Basilicata in the arch of the Italian boot, facing the Gulf of Taranto. There the family name is prominent. A centrepiece of the historic park at the heart of the

With his father Wilson proudly looking on, Emerson signs autographs at the auto show in Sao Paulo at the end of 1970. Soon to celebrate his twenty-fourth birthday, Fittipaldi has returned to Brazil in triumph as the first person from his nation ever to win a Formula 1 Grand Prix.

province is the Palazzo Fittipaldi, dating from the ninth century. Emilio Fittipaldi was prominent in local politics in the 1880s, not far from the time that Emerson's granddad decided to try his luck in Brazil.

Emerson's father Wilson Fittipaldi was born in Sao Paulo; Brazil's industrial city, it was the centre for any automotive activity. The young Wilson was caught up in that milieu. He was a motorcycle racer until active participation was ended by a severe crash in 1952, but Wilson stayed involved with the sport as a reporter and later a radio and television commentator. In this role he'd accompanied the first European sorties of Juan Fangio to Europe in 1948 and '49, broadcasting news of the Argentine's successes to his Portuguese-speaking audiences in South America.

Brazil had her own racing hero in Wilson's time, Francisco 'Chico' Landi. Born in 1907, Landi was four years older than Fangio. After scoring home successes, Landi too sought Europe's brighter lights. With a 2-litre Ferrari he won a Formula 2 race at Bari in 1948, a notable Brazilian success in the Old World. When the Bari race was run for sports cars in 1952, Landi won that as well. Wilson Fittipaldi assisted Landi in his European sorties, which extended into the 1950s with Formula 2 Maseratis, all the while reporting vividly and dramatically to Radio Panamericana. For young Brazilians Chico Landi, successful car builder as well as racer, was an attractive role model. The veteran was still winning races in Brazil in 1964.

'Wilson was a type of Murray Walker in Brazil,' said Jo Ramirez, referring to the famed BBC and ITV Grand Prix presenter. 'He used to commentate on different sports. He was an excellent person,' added Ramirez, who knew the family well. 'I liked him very much. Of the three, he had his feet on the ground the most. He was very good for his two sons; he'd always give them good advice. Their mother was very good with them too.'

'I'm not one-hundred-per cent Latin,' Emerson would later say. 'That is, my father only has a little Italian blood and my mother was born in Russia.' In fact he had a Russian grandmother on his mother's side. Born Juzy Vycikowski in Poland, his mother and her family fled Warsaw for Sao Paulo between the wars. Wilson and Juzy met when both were at university there and married

soon afterwards. Happily, they shared a strong interest in motor racing. In 1951, for example, they teamed up with their friends the Ribeiros to compete in the 24 Hours of Interlagos. While the men placed seventh the ladies were 14th.

'Wilson was wealthy,' said Ramirez, 'but not rich. But they supported their sons in everything they did.' The sons were two in number, starting with Wilson Junior, a Christmas-day baby of 1943. Emerson arrived almost three years later on 12 December 1946. By lucky chance both fell in age groups that were ineligible for Brazil's compulsory military service. At their stylish villa in Sao Paulo's Morumbi district the youngsters were suffused with racing lore: 'He always talked racing at home,' Emerson recalled of his father, so 'since my youngest days I knew what I wanted to do.' One of their most treasured trophies is a shared cup for bicycle-racing victories dating from 1951. Their competitiveness was already under test.

'My father never encouraged us to become racing drivers,' Emerson said. 'Dad gave us a sailboat when Wilson was 16 and I was 13, hoping we'd think about something else. However, it was useless.' Worst of all, they proved to be useless at sailing their Snipe, which had won championships for its previous owner. Instead, when not studying at the Caetano de Campos Institute in Sao Paulo the lads were on wheels, young Wilson on go-karts – which you had to be 17 to race – and his younger brother on motorbikes. In 1962, at the age of 15, Emerson first won a sanctioned race at Interlagos. But for a year he was grounded by mother Juzy, apprehensive over the obvious risks her youngest was running on two wheels.

Motorised water sports were more Emerson's speed. In 1966 he raced an outboard-powered speedboat. 'That was really a fabulous sensation,' he recalled. 'I think it must be one of the most exciting sports there is. You are not in the water, and you are not flying – you are half-way between the two. If you crash in one of those you can injure yourself badly. I gave it up after about four races. I won three, but I didn't want to take risks like that any more.'

Before he was old enough to race go-karts, Emerson was testing, preparing, tuning and building them. 'My father had a beautiful garage at home,' he said, 'with lots of tools, and we could do anything we needed to do on the go-karts. I was very interested in two-stroke engines and how to tune them. I was tuning my brother's and generally it was very successful, winning a lot of races. And I kept his go-kart immaculate. I would look after it, polish the chrome. It was the best on any track.

'That really was the start of my business career,' Emerson told Elizabeth Hayward. 'I was running a little tuning business at home. I was still at school, but I was tuning Wilson's engine and he was winning a lot of races. He won the championship. And then friends of ours started asking me to tune their engines. I had six or seven go-karts to look after, to see that they ran properly. After every weekend's racing they would bring them to the garage and I would strip them down and re-build the engine for the next race. I thought this was fabulous, because it was a way to do what I enjoyed and to get money.'

The tousle-haired younger Fittipaldi was dashing hither and yon, deeply engaged in everything save the most formal schoolwork, battling the heavy acne that left his face ruggedly pock-marked. His dark eyes sparkled with enthusiasm and his upper teeth protruded from a broad smile. He picked up the nickname of 'mouse' in those years. 'I was very small for my age,' he told Mary Schnall Heglar, 'and I was Wilson's mechanic, and I was rushing around, and they said, "Oh, he's coming from everywhere," and they called me *"el rato"* or "mouse." Maybe it's also because of my teeth or because I'm methodical and precise.'

From 1964, as soon as he was eligible, Emerson proved brilliant at karting. He started with a hand-me-down from another budding driver and contemporary of his brother, José Carlos Pace. Following a proven pattern, the boys started making their own machines, which they called 'Mini-karts.' They financed this with some funds that Wilson Jnr. had managed to set aside. 'Dad never gave us a penny,' said Wilson. 'We had to do everything on our own. Emerson was doing really well. He was scintillating on our go-karts, and each of his victories was accompanied by three or four orders for karts!' The prize money was useful, too, added Emerson: 'It is profitable in Brazil, where kart races pay you twice the cost of

building the kart itself. Besides, often it is the only way to keep racing.'

Laid back with a low centre of gravity, the Fittipaldi style was already evident in his karting. 'I like karts very much,' said Emerson. 'It's good for the balance. You can learn how to overtake on braking, how to close the door, and all this does not cost a lot of money. The experience I gained at the beginning of my career on go-karts helped me a lot in controlling cars. I acquired a great deal of sensitivity.' It also brought success and, with that, notoriety. In 125cc karts Emerson won a Sao Paulo championship in 1966 and, in the following year, a national championship. The young man was starting to be noticed, big time.

Nineteen-sixty-seven in fact saw a spectacular double for the precocious youngster. Brazil was the land of the VW Beetle, with a huge factory spewing out the bugs as Brazil's national cars. So when racing for Formula Vees was announced, using VW engines and suspensions, it was a major event. 'We decided to build Formula Vees to sell, not just to race,' Emerson told Elizabeth Hayward. 'We made a special one, a very, very thin one, very aero-dynamic. I was very thin then, and the first one was made for my size. My brother couldn't get in it. It was so nice, like a tailor-made suit,' he said of the cars that they had named 'Fitti-Vees'.

'I think in 1967 there were seven championship races in Brazil,' Emerson continued, 'and I won five in that car. We made about 28 Formula Vees and had only three in our works team; we sold the rest. It was a good business! We did make quite a lot of money during the year, but in the end we lost it all because Formula Vee stopped in Brazil. It lasted just one year, and we had no warning that it would stop. So there we were, with Formula Vee cars, a lot of spare parts and eight people working for us who were suddenly without jobs, so we had to pay them compensation.'

That the brothers could pay off those redundant workers was a consequence of another business that Emerson had started. It was sparked by a small leather-rimmed steering wheel that his brother brought back from a trip to Europe in 1964. This was a new fashion then, inspired by the tiny steering wheels of the latest Formula 1 cars. 'He put it on his car and it was fabulous,' said Emerson. 'Everybody liked it. So I bought a piece of aluminium and some rubber and a piece of leather, and I made one by hand. It took me three days to finish. I sewed it all round, very neat stitches!

'I finished the little steering wheel,' added Emerson, 'and put it on my car and a friend of ours came round and saw it, and he said: "That's a very nice steering wheel! I want to buy it from you!" It gradually became a real business. In 1964 we didn't make a lot, but in 1965 we were making a hundred a month, and I left school because the business was more fun for me. I rented a place, a bigger garage, and had these three people working with me, and when we stopped we were making two hundred a month. It really was a big business, going up all the time.'

'Emerson started to get bored with go-karts,' said his brother, 'and wanted to venture into cars. We didn't have much money, so we thought of touring cars. In 1965 my brother was already at the wheel of a Dauphine Gordini and then an Alpine GT. During his first year he took part in nine races, winning twice, finishing second once, twice fourth and once fifth.' The fifth-place finish was in his first-ever car race on 11 April at a track near Rio.

'We were now buying cars with money from the steering-wheel business,' Emerson said. They'd bought a modified Corvette but this proved more troublesome than successful. The same was true of their next acquisition: 'We sold the Chevy and bought an Alfa Romeo 1300GT, an Alfa Zagato. The car was quite old in Brazil, but very quick, and the first time I took it to Interlagos I went very quickly with that car, the quickest lap.' In 1966 he and Carlos Pace co-drove the pretty but fallible Alfa in a 1,000-kilometre race on the streets of the nation's capital, Brasilia, but had to retire. He salvaged his season with some drives for the works DKW team, whose ring-a-ding two-strokes were familiar ground after all his karting experience.

Also in '66 first Wilson and then Emerson were racing a device called a Karmann-Ghia-Porsche, based on the locally built Karmann-Ghia VW with Porsche power. In their own workshops they built an extremely ambitious prototype powered by a Porsche flat-six and patterned after the then-new 906 or Carrera 6. Swingeing import duties meant that such a car was prohibitively costly to import, so the local Porsche distributor part-sponsored this effort. This, the Fitti-Porsche, they raced in 1967 and '68 but with more DNFs than successes.

Meanwhile the brothers launched yet another business to cater for Beetle drivers wanting more power and performance. 'By this time,' said Emerson, 'for Volkswagens we were making magnesium wheels, special gear ratios, oil radiators to put on the front, and a special fibreglass body. It was exactly the same shape as the normal body. We also made fibreglass bumpers. We even made special long-distance tanks for racing, fibreglass seats, everything for racing. Our firm was called Equipamento Fittipaldi.'

To promote their products they built an ultra-light methanol-fuelled VW 'funny car' of their own, which became justly famous as 'Number 87'. Like the other persimmon-orange Fittipaldi racers, this was backed by Brazil's Bardahl oil-additive company and Varga, the local maker of Girling disc brakes. The brothers co-drove it to victory in a 12-hour race at Porto Alegre in 1968. Underpinning their creations were the mechanical skills of Nelson Enzo Brizzi, a former aviation technician in his late forties. Brizzi had been in charge of preparation for Brazil's Willys-Renault team, for which both brothers had driven. Designer Richard Divila described Brizzi as 'our grand old man of mechanical knowledge, a great "practical" man.'

Divila, a student of aeronautical engineering, was drawn into the Fittipaldi orbit by a mutual interest in cars. When the brothers saw his cutaway drawings of racing cars, they suggested that he design a new racer for them. In 1969 this was taking shape as a Can-Am-style spyder with Alfa Romeo power and a Porsche transaxle when a delay in getting crucial castings meant that it couldn't be ready for the big season-ending 1,000-kilometre race on Rio's Jacarepagua circuit, less than three weeks away. Just as crucially, Fittipaldi rivals were importing heavy machinery for the race, including a GT40 Ford, Chevy-powered Lola and Type 33 Alfa Romeo.

How to respond? The suggestion came from Richard Divila, who had picked up a copy of *Hot Rod* at the airport. Like the latest dragsters, why not build a twin-engined Beetle? With Emerson away racing in Europe,

Wilson Jnr. green-lighted the project and mucked in with Nelson Brizzi, Divila and Deusdedith José de Sena to build a Beetle with two VW engines back-to-back mounted forward of the rear wheels.

Their plan was as simple as it was audacious. Taking one Volkswagen platform, they sliced across it just behind the driver's seat and threw the back part away. Attached to stock VW front suspension and steering were Porsche brakes. To the rear was an all-new tubular frame. Its tubes tied into a rectangular cross-member above the clutch housing that provided mounts for the rear coil/shock spring units. They connected with VW-type swing axles given plenty of negative camber and guided by twin trailing radius arms on each side. Overhung at the rear was a Porsche racing transaxle with only its top four ratios operative.

Darci Medeiros took charge of engine preparation. The front engine was connected to the rear one by a rubber doughnut-type joint. The front crank was phased at 90° to the rear one so the firing sequence would be correct, or nearly so, and all the exhaust pipes were paired, then paired again and brought together at the rear to a single central outlet protruding through the rear deck. Its sound was fantastic, 'like a Porsche 917,' Emerson recalled.

Nominally measuring 1,600cc apiece, the twin engines gave the racer its official name: Fittipaldi-3200. Though run in near-stock tune in their first tests, both engines were later Darci-ised with special cams, higher compression ratio, careful porting and twin Weber 48-mm carburettors. Richard Divila also recalls big cylinders and longer strokes that brought each up to 2,200cc for a total displacement of 4,400cc. Huge jets in the Webers allowed methanol fuel – from a tank that was also the passenger seat – and cooling by a battery of ducts instead of fans.

Made by Glaspac, the Fittipaldis' usual supplier, the glassfibre body was thin-skinned and formed at the rear as a single shell, fenders and all, that hinged up to expose the engine room. Emerson was seated so low that he could barely see over the cowl. The rear-view mirror had to be raised so he could see it through the Plexiglas side window with its sliding vent. Much taller, Wilson didn't have that problem. Jammed under the fenders were Firestone Indy tyres on special wide magnesium rims, holding up a car that weighed just under 900 pounds.

Incredibly, there was time to test the eight-cylinder 'Bug' at Interlagos before the Rio race. Just back from Europe, Emerson took its wheel. Amazed at what his colleagues had wrought, he was even more astonished when he pushed for lap times. Behind him was the deafening roar of eight air-cooled cylinders and the wind wailed around him as the tops of the flimsy doors blew open. But this mobile masquerade was turning quicker lap times than those of Brazil's fastest race-prepared touring cars. Emerson couldn't stop laughing. The whole thing was just too impossibly hilarious. It was incredible, improbably, utterly Brazilian and too funny to be true.

Rio's Jacarepagua track, however, would tell the story. Twisty and bumpy, its road circuit was attached to a mildly-banked oval track, laid out on a flat, sun stricken plain near the Atlantic coast and famous for the poorest crowd control in Latin America. White-garbed ice cream vendors, with huge sling-suspended containers, deserted their pitches on the famous beaches at Rio to sell their wares at Jacarepagua, strolling on the race-car side of the pit wall and crossing the track to slake the thirsts of corner workers.

Artfully dodging these and other hazards, Carlos Pace set fastest qualifying time at 1:30.9 in the Alfa Romeo Type 33. Second fastest, at 1:36.3, was none other than the Fittipaldi-3200, clocked by Wilson. Third was a Porsche-type special and fourth, at 1:40.0, was a Chevy-engined Lola Type 70 coupé. It was followed by a Ford GT40, up to date with Weslake-type cylinder heads, at 1:41.4. That had to be the first time that anything resembling a Volkswagen qualified faster than those great cars on any track in the world.

Nobody expected the roaring orange Beetle to survive 100 kilometres, let alone 1,000, but it was sensational while it lasted. Emerson was the starting driver, his helmet barely visible over its window sills. The cheeky 'Bug' was in third place when the field completed its first lap. By lap five it moved up to second, behind the Alfa, easily holding off the Lola and the GT40. But after less than half an hour Emerson was in the pits. Gearbox problems ended their audacious effort.

'After that race,' said Emerson, 'I received a phone call from someone at Volkswagen, asking if they could send someone to our shops. The next day eight engineers came to look at the car. They said, "We just couldn't understand how a Volkswagen could outrace a Lola-Chevrolet, so we were sent down here to see." After they saw the car they still couldn't believe it!' It raced a few more times before being scrapped. On one occasion, said Emerson, 'The whole car started to come apart at the same time!'

The story of the Fittipaldi-3200 is edifying as an exemplar of the irrepressible enthusiasm and determination of Brazilians in general and the Fittipaldis in particular. It also formed a stepping stone toward Emerson's future career, for Darci Medeiros would come to Europe in 1970 to assist Fittipaldi's successful Lotus Formula 2 campaign. Richard Divila, who had already been in Britain with Emerson in '69, would return in 1970 and would later design the first Fittipaldi Grand Prix cars.

His international commitments meant that Emerson would race less in Brazil in the future, save for the all-important Brazilian Grands Prix. On 29 February 1970 he had the honour of winning the first race on the revived Interlagos track. First opened in 1940, Interlagos had fallen into disrepair during the 1950s and was only rebuilt to an international standard at the end of the 1960s. The 1970 race was the last of six events of a special Brazilian Formula Ford series with equal cars and top European drivers. It meant a special challenge for Emerson, who had returned to Sao Paulo as Lombank Formula 3 champion: 'There was a lot of pressure on me. I *had* to win the series. In Brazil people expected me to win Formula Ford so easily. They would not have understood if I should not win.'

'I did win the series for Brazil,' Emerson told Elizabeth Hayward, 'but it was really hard work. I won four out of the six races. The build-up of publicity had been terrific, so by the time we got to the last race at Sao Paulo the crowd was enormous, as big as if it were a Formula 1 race.' Emerson met their expectations with his win at the refurbished Interlagos. 'After that my country expected a great deal of me. Every detail of my career – every race, everything I did – was reported in the Brazilian news-papers.'

At the end of 1970 their expectations were even higher. By then Emerson was a Grand-Prix winner, after all. For the Brazil Cup, a series of sports-car races, he chose a 1.8-litre Lola T210 to compete against Can-Am cars and a Ferrari 512, reasoning that the newness of the light Lola would score against those bigger but older cars. It was a shrewd gamble; he won the series.

Another Brazilian series with imported Formula 2 cars and drivers was organised for October and November of 1971. Driving a Team Bardahl Lotus 69, Fittipaldi dominated this four-round *Torneio Brasiliano* with wins in the first two races at Interlagos and a second at Porto Alegre. Another similar *Torneio* was laid on at the same time in 1972. Emerson won the first race, Carlos Pace the second and Mike Hailwood the third – all at Interlagos. After a track inspection the final race at Porto Alegre was cancelled, and Fittipaldi was declared the series winner on points.

If Brazil's previous expectations for Emerson had been high, they were astronomical when he came back for the 1972 *Torneio*. Now he was the Grand Prix World Champion, the youngest in history. He was the 'mouse' who roared.

The Brazilian arm of oil-additive producer Bardahl backs Emerson from his first days in the sport. When he hits the big time, Bardahl publishes an advertisement that gives credit to the young man's early races on karts and production cars and chronicles his rise to the top.

Emerson começa em 62, correndo escondido.
Nem mamãe sabia disto.

Em 63, recebe o seu primeiro prêmio.
Tinha apenas 15 anos e uma moto.

64. Várias vitórias com kart.
E com Bardahl.

O primeiro carro, um Renault R 8.
Estréia em 64, na Ilha do Fundão, GB.

Emerson venceu este "pega" e a corrids.
Era o ano de 1966.

Em 67, vitória nas "3 Horas de Velocidade", GB.
Com um Karmann Ghia / Porsche.

Um campeão de Norte a Sul. Nas "12 Horas de
Porto Alegre", com Wilsinho, ainda em 67.

Em 68, Emerson passa para a Fórmula V.
V de vitória. Várias.

Quando os sucessos no Brasil começam a virar
rotina, Emerson vai para a Europa.
E a rotina continua. 1969.

No mesmo ano, o Grande Prêmio da Inglaterra
de Fórmula III fica para inglês ver.

Em 70, vai para a Lotus. Mas fica
pouquíssimo na Fórmula II. Motivo: várias
vitórias só no 1.º semestre.

Emerson fazendo a América. Estréia na
Fórmula I e vence o Grande Prêmio dos EE.UU.

No fim deste ano, Emerson volta
ao país para um passeio em Interlagos:
é o 1.º na Copa Brasil.

Na campanha de 71, ele fica em 6.º
Por isso, um projeto ambicioso,
o Lotus-Turbina, é abandonado.

Em 72, um gesto comum na Europa:
Emerson vence na Bélgica,
Inglaterra, Áustria, Espanha...

... até a consagração total
como Campeão do Mundo, por antecipação,
no G.P. da Itália.

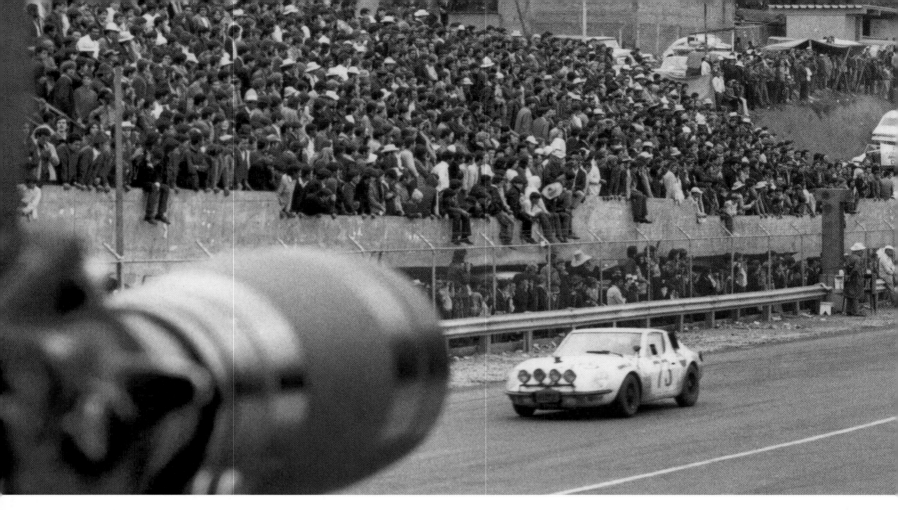

The crowd swamping the main straight at Interlagos for a race in 1970 gives a hint of the enthusiasm of Emerson's fellow Brazilians for the sport of motor racing (top). They soon expect miracles from young Fittipaldi. Emerson joins his brother Wilson Jnr. at the Sao Paulo auto show in 1968 (left). The car-crazy brothers get into the accessory business through Emerson's steering wheels and soon produce equipment for vehicles up to and including racing Volkswagen Beetles (right).

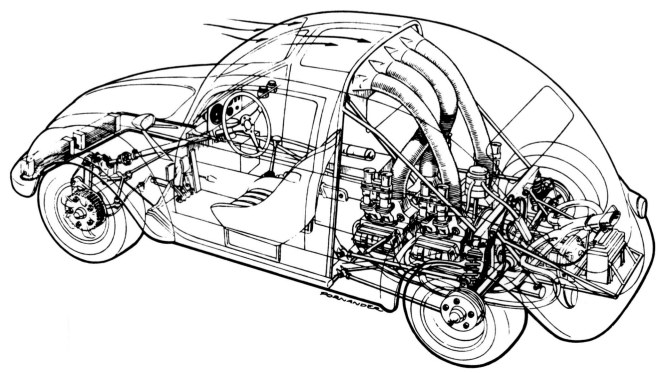

Among the amazing creations of the Fittipaldi brothers is the 'Bug that Roared', a plastic-bodied Beetle powered by a midship-mounted eight-cylinder engine made up of Volkswagen parts. A slot in its front bumper contains oil coolers while engine-cooling air is ducted above the windscreen over the driver's head (left). After tests at Interlagos (above) Emerson races it at Rio (opposite) where it embarrasses some very expensive machinery. Even after they see it, VW's engineers can't believe it.

CHAPTER 3

'Emerson Who?'

'We were a bunch of kids,' Richard Divila recalled of 1969, Emerson's first summer abroad. 'In July we went to the British Grand Prix in a clapped-out Ford Cortina. That was our hotel. And the next year Emerson was on the grid there in a Lotus 49!' Such was the sudden rise to racing prominence of the youngster from Sao Paulo.

'At a certain point I realised I'd nothing more to say in Brazil. South America wasn't the Mecca of motor racing.' That's how Emerson recalled his decision to chance his luck and skill abroad. England seemed the obvious place to go. But was it? Although Wilson had already raced abroad, he had no leads to offer. He'd competed in Europe in a Formula 3 Pygmée during the 1965 and '66 seasons, albeit with slight success.

Many counselled that Italy was the best choice – Italy, ancestral land of the Fittipaldis, and not short of racing opportunities at the end of the 1960s. 'I knew the

Keen as the proverbial mustard, Emerson Fittipaldi is hailed in Europe as 'the amazing flying coffee bean'. Although a newcomer to racing European-style, he arrives in the Old World after thousands of kilometres of tough competition in Brazil.

language quite well but I didn't know any English,' Emerson recalled. 'Then there was Ferrari, my great dream.' However, prospects in England looked brighter, and after a talk with Jerry Cunningham, an expat Brit who was a partner in Glaspac, the company that supplied the Fittipaldis with plastic Beetle bodies, Cunningham said he'd introduce him to Dennis Rowland, who built Formula Ford engines. With this encouragement, Emerson plumped for Britain.

Financing his venture was entirely up to Emerson. 'We had put some money away selling go-karts and driving in Formula Vee races,' he recalled. 'I decided to take all my money out. However, I realised I needed more. I didn't think twice. I had a car that I sold to the best bidder.' 'Emerson sold everything,' recalled Richard Divila. 'He sold his watch, his Porsche engine and the 911 that he was planning to race.' 'I calculated that I had enough money to buy a Formula Ford and to live on for three months,' said Fittipaldi. 'I had enough to tempt fate. But I had no time to lose. I had to do everything in a hurry!'

This money problem was not minor, even for an effort in the lowest formula. 'Anybody in racing in Brazil had *some* money,' explained Richard Divila. 'But a reasonably well-off Brazilian is quite poor in Europe. And to move out of that warm atmosphere, to go to another world – especially the Anglo-Saxon world – is not easy. That's why those Brazilians who *do* manage it tend to do well.'

'I got on the first plane with a return ticket in my pocket, enough money to buy a racing car and a little to live on,' said Emerson. Imagine the impact of that transition! From the sunshine of vibrant Brazil to a dank, grey London in a land where he knew few and could speak to none save Jerry Cunningham, who accompanied him. It was even colder and windier in Norfolk, where he saw his first motor race in the Old World: 'Snetterton was the first track I saw in Europe. The first weekend we arrived in England, Jerry said that there was a club meeting on there and we went to look. It was February, and it was *freezing*.'

Fittipaldi's campaign was unpretentious. 'He drove the car everywhere himself,' said Divila, 'on a trailer with an old clapped-out Land Rover.' 'The only person I knew there back then was Frank Williams,' said Emerson, 'but he didn't have a Titan to sell me, so I went to Merlyn. I bought a Mark 11A and got an engine for the car from Dennis Rowland.'

The introduction to Rowland was fortuitous. In addition to allowing Emerson to base his Merlyn at Wimbledon, in his parents' garage, Rowland put the Brazilian to work. 'I owe him a lot,' Emerson said later, 'as he gave me the opportunity to earn a few more pounds and learn about competition engines.' The 22-year-old already knew a lot about competition engines, but the Formula Ford fours were new to him. He learned a lot more about them after his first race at Zandvoort on 7 April: 'I was in the lead when I heard a horrible knocking sound behind me – it was the engine giving up. I thought my European adventure was already at an end, as I didn't have enough money to buy another engine.'

Rowland to the rescue: 'He made me an interesting proposal. He would give me the spare parts free if I helped him in the workshop. I accepted, as I had no other choice and I didn't want to return to Brazil empty-handed.' Repairs completed, they took the Merlyn to Snetterton for a shakedown. 'While enjoying the pleasure of speed again, I heard a dull thud in the gearbox.' A shaft

had sheared. 'We went back to Wimbledon. Dennis was very upset. That day I cried. I really thought I would go back to Brazil, because you work so hard and so long, and then something stupid happens.'

Rowland was instrumental in persuading Emerson to persevere. The next race at Snetterton was his break-through. Peter Swinger wrote that he remembered well 'a day he was flag marshalling at the second Ess on the original Snetterton when an orange Formula Ford appeared from under the Bailey bridge at a most peculiar angle. The same antic was performed the next lap and the yellow flag was readied as this tyro was clearly headed for disaster. But he continued in this manner and was obviously in complete control of the situation and went on to win the first of many races. His name was Emerson Fittipaldi and the rest, as the saying goes, is history.' 'I was happy then,' said Emerson. 'Winning that race meant a lot to me because my morale went up a lot, after all the disappointment and hard work. I carried on racing with Dennis for another eight races and I won another two.'

In *Motor* of 9 August 1969 a photo appeared of a very youthful-looking Emerson in a Jim Russell Formula Ford. Philip Turner explained: 'The Jim Russell Inter-national Racing Drivers' School are to expand their racing programme for Formula 3, and are to enter a Lotus 59 in major British and Continental F3 races. The driver will be the young Brazilian, Emerson Fittipaldi, who began racing in Brazil in 1965 when he won the Rio de Janeiro championship with a Renault Gordini R8. In 1966 he won the Sao Paulo karting championship and in 1967 won both the Brazilian karting and Formula Vee championships. This season, he has competed in eight Formula Ford races with a Merlyn 11A, winning three and never finishing lower than fourth.'

Turner's précis of the Fittipaldi career helped explain his remarkable early success in Europe. His was a wise racing head on young shoulders. 'Emerson was already a seasoned veteran when he went over there,' said Richard Divila. 'He had driven for the Willys-Renault works team. He'd competed in long-distance races. With that and his karting he'd learned a lot of racecraft. Until then, however, he was in the shadow of older drivers like Wilson, Carlos Pace and Luis Bueno.' Now, with Jim

Russell, he stepped smartly out of the shadow and into the limelight of Formula 3.

The Russell connection was engineered by a mutual friend, Brazilian Carlos Avallone. Wrote Doug Nye, 'Russell offered him a deal whereby he sold his Formula Ford Merlyn and bought a Lotus 59 rolling chassis. Mike Warner of Lotus Components helped to arrange an engine.' Warner ran Components separately from the rest of Group Lotus to build Sevens and cars for lesser Formulas, allowing Colin Chapman to concentrate on his Grand Prix and road cars. Emerson regarded the Russell connection positively: 'I think Jim was very good for me. He is a good businessman.

'I was very excited to move to Formula 3 so soon,' Emerson told Elizabeth Hayward, 'and to be connected with Lotus even in this little way. I had my car by July, in time for Mallory Park, my first race in Formula 3.' If not exactly poisoned, however, the chalice brimmed with a bitter draught. 'Everybody said the car, the Lotus 59, was very bad.' Emerson recalled. The same Dave-Baldwin-designed tube-framed chassis was used for Formulas 2 and 3, and in the lesser series the 59's spring rates, oil tank and aerodynamics needed work. This was meat and drink to the Brazilian, who now had a chance to apply his chassis-tuning skills.

His first race in the 59 was in July at Mallory Park, where he finished fifth. At Brands he was second and at Mallory again, in his third Formula 3 race, Emerson was the winner. 'I think I won the next seven races,' he said. 'Out of eleven races in Formula 3 I won eight, all in Jim Russell's Lotus 59.' One he didn't win was a September Bank Holiday meeting at Brands Hatch. Emerson set fastest practice time and won his heat ahead of Ronnie Peterson. He was leading in the final when oil on the track started some back markers spinning. Fittipaldi raised his hand to warn drivers behind him, only to spin on the oil. He regained his poise to finish third behind Reine Wisell and Tim Schenken. In *Motor* Doug Nye wrote, 'Wisell's was a brilliant win, which so easily could have gone to any four other drivers. Fittipaldi underlined his promise with a skilful and very sporting performance.'

Against future Grand Prix drivers Peterson, Wisell and Schenken, the F3 series was hard-fought. Another competitor in that championship, Charles Lucas, wrote of 'the amazing "flying coffee bean" Emerson Fittipaldi … about to be launched on an incredulous public.' In October the bean bounced over the Channel, as Philip Turner reported: 'Once again that astonishing Brazilian driver, Emerson Fittipaldi, dominated a Formula 3 race from start to finish. This time it was the Coupe de Salon at Montlhéry which the Brazilian won from Mazet and Jaussaud in Tecnos.'

In the final round of the Lombank Championship on the Brands Hatch club circuit Emerson had to collect points if he were to prevail. In a wet race two rivals took the lead. Emerson had no answer, he told Elizabeth Hayward: 'I was driving right on the limit. I could not have gone faster. Then both of them spun off, so I was again in the lead and I won the race – and the Lombank Championship. My father was broadcasting this live, to Brazil, and they all teased me about my interview after the race. I said: "I am happy. We are happy. I think we are all happy!"'

Not only was Emerson's father in England; his mother had arrived as well during the summer to see that her youngest was properly fed and watered at the house they rented near Norwich. Other friends came to add support as his star swung to the zenith. In *Motor* of 25 October 1969 Philip Turner wrote: 'Not surprisingly, Emerson Fittipaldi has been snatched up by Lotus to lead their Formula 3 team, and to drive in Formula 2 as well. Fittipaldi, who is on a two-year contract with Lotus, hit the headlines only late this season with some dramatic drives in which he challenged and sometimes beat the established F3 kings like Peterson, Wisell and Schenken.'

In fact Emerson's 1970 season in Europe saw him desert Formula 3 for the more senior class, for which Dave Baldwin had designed a new semi-monocoque car to take the newly mandatory bag-type fuel tanks. This, the Lotus 69, was powered by the ubiquitous 1.6-litre Cosworth-Ford FVA four. Moving up so quickly to Formula 2 was a huge step for Fittipaldi, and in career terms a successful one. 'Without a doubt,' he told Gordon Kirby, 'that was the most important stage in my racing career. The timing and sequence of events couldn't have been better for me, it was because of good luck and people like Jim Russell and Ralph Firman. All the ingredients were right, the timing was perfect and luck was on my side.'

However, his best efforts couldn't buy a win for Emerson in Formula 2 in 1970. He was competing against established stars like Jochen Rindt, Jackie Stewart, Jacky Ickx and Graham Hill, who raced in the lower formula as well as Formula 1. In their company, however, he could have had no better schooling in Europe's tracks and tactics. 'In my opinion Formula 2 races are very important,' he said, 'because they enable you to refine your driving skills and get in a great deal of practice. It's useful training.' In a dozen races his best finish was a second at Imola. This plus a handsome handful of thirds and fourths placed him third in the eight-race European Formula 2 championship for non-graded drivers behind Gianclaudio 'Clay' Regazzoni and Derek Bell.

Emerson was less active in 1971's F2 season, but he did compete in a Team Bardahl Lotus 69 alongside his brother in some events. He was second in the Eifelrennen, then won at Jarama. *Motor* reported on his next race in leafy London: 'In front of a holiday crowd estimated at nearly 20,000, the Brazilian driver Emerson Fittipaldi made it two in a row by winning the Hilton Transport International Trophy race at Crystal Palace. For Emerson Fittipaldi it was a great triumph.' He won again at Albi at the end of September in a car that he and Richard Divila had developed during the year, discovering a need to set its roll centres precisely. 'Although bound to the car by contract,' said Doug Nye in his Lotus history, 'he got on with the job in hand in his characteristically quiet and intelligent manner and sorted it out into a race-winner.'

Emerson kept his hand in Formula 2, in 1973 driving a Lotus called the 'Texaco Star,' Ralph Bellamy's first design for Lotus. A harbinger of its future was the first car's bursting into flames at Snetterton with Fittipaldi at the wheel. If Emerson was appearing less often in Formula 2 it was for a very good reason. He'd been talent-spotted by the other team at Hethel, Lotus's base near Norfolk. His first contact with Colin Chapman was at the December, 1969 end-of-season Lotus luncheon, where Mike Warner introduced the Brazilian to his chief. 'He just about said "Hello, how are you?" totally

without interest,' Emerson recalled. 'I don't suppose he really knew who I was at that time. I went back to Brazil for the winter, convinced that my adventure at Lotus was over.

'I returned to Britain in March,' Fittipaldi continued, 'and went to Lotus Components one day to see what was going on. Chapman was coming out of the gate in his Elan Plus Two. He stopped right in front of me and without getting out said, "Hi, Fittipaldi. I'd like you to do some Formula 1 testing for us. What do you think?" I nearly fell down! Imagine, after all my dreams, Colin Chapman actually asking me to sit in one of his Formula 1 cars. It was too much.' The Team Lotus scene had changed since the previous year; Graham Hill had left to drive for Rob Walker and all Chapman's chips were on Jochen Rindt. A second Lotus seat could be open for the right racer.

In May 1970 Emerson joined Chapman in his private plane for the flight to Silverstone for a test session. Rindt was there with the still-new 72 and next to it was the 49C that the Austrian had just driven to victory at Monaco. 'I was very worried,' said Emerson, 'as I was afraid something would go wrong. I knew Chapman was very demanding. He works hard and wants everyone else that works with him to work hard. If I'd driven slowly he wouldn't have appreciated me. If I'd driven fast I might have ended up against the barriers and ruined everything. I still remember those hours as a nightmare.

'It was like a re-birth, those first laps,' Fittipaldi told Elizabeth Hayward. 'I just couldn't believe that I was driving the winning car from Monaco, and Colin was watching. I found it was much easier to drive than I expected. The 49 was a very forgiving car. Even from the beginning I could drive it very close to the limit. The car was understeering a lot, and I brought it in and told them I thought we needed more front wing because the car was understeering a lot in the corners. And they *knew* this. They had set it up especially to understeer to see if I noticed and could tell them what to do. They did it on purpose! So they put on more front wing and I went out again.

'The next lap when I came by I saw Jochen giving me the time,' continued Emerson. ' He was just so excited by the times I was doing that he took the signal board from the mechanics and held it out for me himself. I think that was fabulous of him. He wasn't jealous, he was just very pleased that I was going quickly. When I came in at the end, Colin was smiling and Dick Scammell was pleased, and they said: "Very good, you have done a good time." And I was *really* happy.'

Testing was one thing, racing another. An approach by Frank Williams was the catalyst, Emerson said: 'Frank Williams's offer was more tempting than Colin's! He offered me more money, and I was very keen to drive for Frank. But I had to ask Colin first. And Colin said, "I am keeping a Formula 1 car for you, there's no problem. I'll sign a contract with you." So we signed a contract for 1970 and 1971. I knew that for my future it was more important to drive for Lotus.' Chapman was keen for the 23-year-old to start at once but Emerson demurred: 'I felt I didn't have enough experience. I felt I needed more experience in Formula 2.'

His début came in the British Grand Prix at Brands Hatch in July. Although the three Lotus 49s filled the back row of the grid, showing their age, Emerson's was the fastest ahead of Graham Hill and American Pete Lovely. He drove a steady race to place eighth, lapped twice by winner Rindt. Retirements marred the German GP at Hockenheim in August, but Fittipaldi was able to take advantage with an excellent fourth place on the same lap as winner Rindt. Biddable the 49 might be, said Emerson, but not easy: 'The 49 was a very heavy car to drive. At the end of the 1970 German GP I couldn't even open my fingers, I'd held the steering wheel so tight!' Still in the old 49C, and despite a good grid position at Austria's Österreichring, he had to refuel and was placed 15th and last.

Next was the Italian GP at Monza on 6 September, where Jochen Rindt could clinch his World Championship. Emerson arrived in Italy doubly blessed. Lotus team manager Peter Warr had confirmed his status as number two in the team to Rindt for the 1971 season. As well, for the first time Emerson would drive one of the new doorstop-shaped 72s, in fact the very latest chassis. In the early laps of Friday practice, he wrecked it.

Afterwards, Eoin Young quizzed Fittipaldi about his crash on the approach to the fast Monza Parabolica. 'He said he and Giunti in the Ferrari had been slipstreaming each other and Giunti was ahead as they approached the braking area,' Young reported. 'Emerson was about to slip out and go alongside Giunti when he glanced in his mirrors to see John Surtees about to do the same thing. In that split second when he had to revise his plans, the Fittipaldi Lotus was committed to climb the rear wheels of the Ferrari.' 'I remember very well the back of the Ferrari!' said Emerson. 'I was going much quicker than he was and I realised I was going to crash. I have a photograph of the Lotus flying over the Ferrari about six feet in the air.'

Emerson would not have raced at Monza in any case, for Lotus's entries were withdrawn after Jochen Rindt's fatal crash into and under the Armco barriers during Saturday practice. 'It was as if the world had collapsed around me,' said Fittipaldi. 'I'd learnt to appreciate Jochen, as he was a real friend. It was a very sad time for everyone at Lotus.' The distraught team regrouped, missing the Canadian GP to prepare for the following race at Watkins Glen. To partner Emerson, Lotus signed Swede Reine Wisell, who had been going well in both Formula 3 and Formula 5000.

Chapman had specific instructions for Emerson at the Glen. Rindt could be the posthumous World Champion if Ferrari-mounted Ickx, in particular, could be denied points. 'Colin came to me before the race and told me: "Emerson, whatever you do you must finish in front of the Ferraris because of the Championship." For me it was funny. I know my limits. I am not *kamikaze*. I told him I would do what I could. It was a great responsibility, and when near the end they told me from the pit that Ickx was coming back at me, I had to accelerate even more, even taking some risks cornering. They didn't tell me he was on my tail, but a lap down!

'It was hard for us to believe that *this* was the track for the United States Grand Prix,' said Fittipaldi of the slippery, gloomy and cold Glen circuit. 'There was mud everywhere on the track. They let us have three or four warming-up laps and I could scarcely believe that this was America, so modern and so rich.' He had excelled in practice with the third-fastest lap, behind the dreaded Ickx on the pole. Emerson could do nothing about the Belgian's Ferrari, but at mid-race Ickx had to stop for fuel-system repairs and Fittipaldi moved to third behind Stewart in the new Tyrrell and the BRM of Pedro Rodriguez.

The Tyrrell retired, handing the lead to Rodriguez. 'As the Yardley BRM team prepared for its second celebration of the year,' reported *Motor*, 'the diminutive Mexican made an unscheduled stop for fuel – it was the 101st lap [of 108]. He had been told by his pit crew that his margin over Fittipaldi was 38 seconds when in reality it was more like 18 or 19. The 20 seconds consumed in the pits allowed the young Brazilian to vault into the lead as Rodriguez floundered helplessly to cross the line more than a half-minute down.'

'With nine laps to go they gave me P1,' said Emerson, 'and I looked behind me because I thought the signal must be for someone else! Then with eight laps to go they gave me P1 again. All the lap I had been thinking they must have made a mistake. I was first! I was leading the race! I could win my first Grand Prix. My mind started to work overtime. I thought of the petrol. Would there be enough? Then I thought about all the components of my Lotus. What would break? The last laps seemed to last forever. Then I saw the chequered flag. I saw Chapman throw his hat in the air. It was for me! I had seen many photographs of Chapman throwing his hat in the air in happiness, first for Jimmy Clark, then Graham Hill and Jochen Rindt. And now it was for me. When I stopped at the pit I couldn't remember a word of English.'

If the outcome was a stunner for the winner, it was stupefying for the rest of the Grand Prix world. 'The US Grand Prix result was one of the great motor racing surprises of the decade,' Philip Turner wrote. Americans outdid themselves in their amazement over this victory in their big race by an unknown Brazilian with an exotic name. 'Emerson Who?' they asked rhetorically. It was a healing catharsis for Team Lotus. Colin Chapman was literally in tears, and the team's Dick Scammell was almost as speechless as Emerson: 'Winning at the Glen was just like a fairy tale … it was too good to be true … we couldn't believe it.'

Not only that, but in his first-ever Grand Prix Reine Wisell was third in this richest of all GP races. Emerson's win paid $50,000 while Wisell's finish brought a welcome $12,000. The year's final race in Mexico was anticlimactic, the Lotuses unhappy with the Mexico City altitude and Emerson qualifying poorly after engine problems and retiring early.

Looking to 1971, Colin Chapman mulled his options. 'I had to decide whether to leave Emerson all the responsibility of being number one,' he said, 'or employ another driver and leave Fittipaldi to gain experience without any worries. I chose to stick with the same two men with whom I'd finished the 1970 season.' Philip Turner summed up the situation: 'Lotus have Emerson Fittipaldi and Wisell under contract for next year, but might run three cars should a top driver join them as number one. It strikes me whoever he is, he will have to be pretty swift to stay ahead of Emerson.' He was not the only one to conclude that this young man was pretty special.

After slipping off his loafers Emerson tries on a Lotus 59. His expression belies the speed with which he rockets from Formula Ford through Formulas 3 and 2 to find both Frank Williams and Colin Chapman keen to engage him for Formula 1.

Emerson still wears his Willys works-team overalls when he arrives in Europe to do battle in Formula Ford. He loses so much weight on the English food that his mother soon arrives to fatten him up. Fittipaldi races a Lotus 49 in the 1970 British Grand Prix (opposite top), conferring before the race with mechanic Herbie Blash, and by October is racing a Lotus 72 at Watkins Glen (opposite bottom). He stuns the racing world by taking the Lotus to a surprise victory in the Glen's 1970 United States Grand Prix (overleaf).

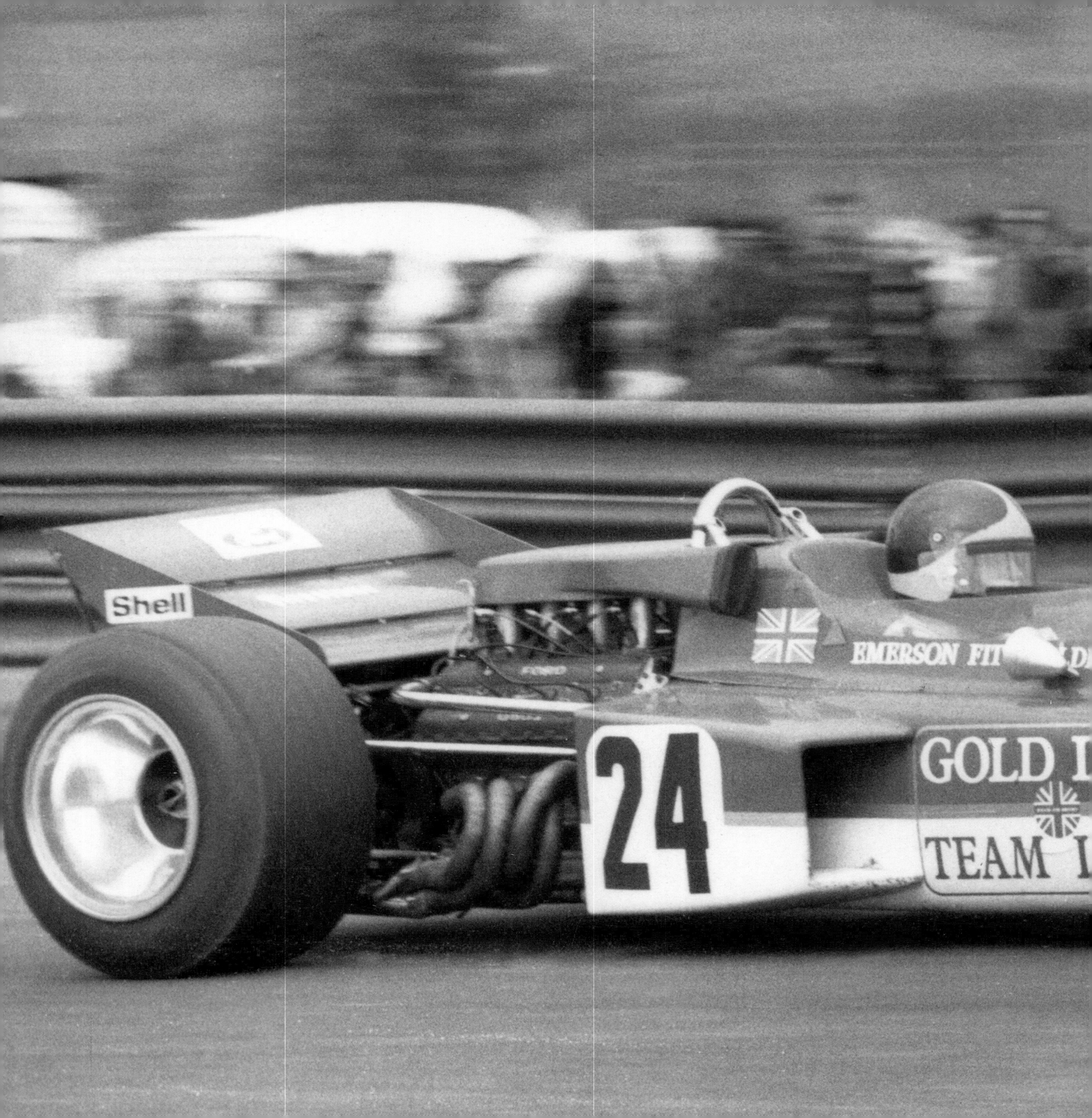
Shell
EMERSON FIT
24
GOLD
TEAM

CHAPTER 4

Youngest Champion

'I have always referred to 1971 as "the year of the turbine",' wrote Elizabeth Hayward, the *nom de plume* of Priscilla Phipps, who was timer and scorer for Team Lotus. 'Frankly I have held the opinion that Colin jeopardised his future relationship with Emerson, his prestige and the morale of the team by persevering with an idea that was fabulous in theory, and just didn't work in practice.'

In practice it sort of worked, but Colin Chapman's unique and unprecedented attempt to make a gas turbine power a Grand Prix car unquestionably undermined his team's 1971 world-championship effort. The result was that for the first time since 1960 Lotus failed to win a single Grand Prix. 'We spent from the end of 1970 to the end of 1971 testing that car,' Emerson said of the turbine-powered 56B. 'That was bad for the Formula 1 programme.' It was also risky, he added: 'Five times the suspension broke while I was driving that car.'

From the conning tower of his Lotus 72, aka John Player Special, Emerson attends to advice from Team Lotus manager Peter Warr. Together they achieve a World Championship in 1972 and the runner-up spot in 1973.

Fittipaldi gave the Lotus turbine its race début in the Race of Champions at Brands in March, 1971. Based on the wedge-shaped Lotus 56 that almost won the Indianapolis 500 in 1968, its Pratt & Whitney turbine was modified to meet the FIA's regulations for such engines. Although he qualified respectably, Emerson never figured in the race, the kerosene-laden racer 'bottoming all round the circuit,' said Doug Nye, 'showering sparks as it graunched and ground over the bumps.' One of the five suspension failures retired it.

Another suspension breakage stopped Fittipaldi's turbine in another non-championship race, this at Silverstone in May. Emerson was deeply disappointed with his second-lap exit in the first heat after having qualified the whooshing racer in the front row, an onlooker saying that 'he seemed to cope with the turbo lag pretty well, and the sheets of flame exiting just behind his head on the entry to Stowe left us, and the marshals, pretty impressed.' Repaired for the second heat, Fittipaldi's turbine scythed through the field from the back row to finish third – but nowhere on aggregate for the International Trophy after his aborted first heat.

Technically orientated as he was, Emerson had a love-hate relationship with the Lotus turbine. 'It was a very difficult car to drive,' he said, 'very, very difficult. We knew we would have to do a lot of development on that car to make it competitive, but it never gave good results.' It had two last chances in 1971, one of them in a championship Grand Prix at Monza. There the hot weather didn't suit the turbine and Emerson struggled, finishing eighth, and a lap behind. Its final outing was in a September non-points race at Hockenheim, where Fittipaldi set fastest lap and finished second in a mixed field.

Abortive and time-consuming though the Lotus turbine was, that 8th of May at Silverstone it gave Emerson his first real form of the 1971 season. Until then he'd struggled. His Grand Prix year started with a non-championship Formula 1 race at Buenos Aires. Because an engine shortage had annulled Lotus's plans to test pre-season, practice there was Emerson's first experience of his 72 with Firestone's new low-profile tyres. He was appalled by the dodgy handling of a car that had worked so well in 1970. 'One of the few times I spun a car was in Argentina,' he told Elizabeth Hayward. 'I had never spun in Formula 2 or Formula 1 since I'd started racing, and this was the first time because I was trying too hard to drive the car quickly, and it just didn't handle.' He struggled to 10th in his heat with expiring oil pressure.

'I went back to Lotus to speak to Maurice Philippe about it, and I told him the car was impossible,' said Emerson. 'He wanted to know how it could be so good in 1970 and how I, as a new driver, could possibly know. I couldn't tell him why it was wrong.' That his colleagues knew something was wrong was evident, as Philip Turner wrote after the Argentine race: 'The Lotus team were terribly puzzled by the odd handling of their 72s and are now busy collecting and studying all the photographs they can lay hands on of the cars in action.'

Nevertheless Lotus chief Chapman was not convinced. He felt 'my bloody drivers' were at fault. 'Reine and I were still so new to Formula 1 racing,' said Fittipaldi, 'that Colin just didn't believe us. When we were explaining a problem to him we had a job to convince him that it was a real one and not simply our lack of experience. On top of this Colin was really more

interested in the turbine car.' His Lotuses were right out of it and unreliable to boot in the Grands Prix of South Africa and Spain and a non-championship race at California's Ontario Motor Speedway.

The California race gave the team its first chance of extensive testing. This led to rear-suspension changes that improved the cars at Monaco for the 23 May race. From next to last on the 18-car grid, Emerson 'drove all through the race, from about lap four, with no clutch and no first gear.' A measure of his determination was his fifth-place finish, a lap behind but his first points of 1971.

At the end of the month Emerson raced and won in Formula 2 at Crystal Palace. The next day, 1 June, he and his wife Maria Helena packed up their new Ford Capri and set out for Lausanne, where they were renting a flat to take up Swiss residence for the first time. Especially for Maria Helena, who was three months' pregnant, it was a big new adventure for the Fittipaldis. The Lake Geneva air would be better for her asthma. After leaving the Autoroute, not far from Dijon, they were about to overtake a slow-moving blue car on a local road when its driver suddenly began turning left. When he heard Fittipaldi's squealing tyres behind him, the Frenchman stopped turning – and the Capri, which had been trying to dodge round his rear, struck him heavily.

Maria Helena's jaw and some teeth were broken. Though carried to term, her baby would be stillborn. Impaled by the steering wheel, Emerson had three broken ribs and two fractures of the sternum, one of which struck an artery in his chest. Taken by ambulance to Dijon, they were flown to Lausanne the next day with the help of Peter Warr and Jackie Stewart.

Emerson wanted to race at Zandvoort three weeks later but his doctors refused permission. Instead he made his comeback at the new Paul Ricard circuit on 4 July, heavily bandaged to hold his thorax in place. He fought the pain to move up through the field in the improved 72 to finish third in the French GP, half a minute behind winner Stewart. 'Fittipaldi's performance was particularly good,' wrote Michael Bowler; 'working out race times against practice times as a percentage, his performance was probably the most consistent.'

Emerson was third again in the next race, Silverstone's British GP, after making a terrible start from an excellent fourth on the grid. He retired at the Nürburgring but was placed second in Austria behind Jo Siffert's BRM, which was slowing with a puncture but not enough to gift him a fortunate win like Watkins Glen's.

Returning to North America, Lotus had no wet-weather suspension settings for a Canadian Grand Prix that started in heavy rain and ended after 60 of the 80-lap race when mist stopped play. Fittipaldi was a dogged seventh. He was 20th and non-classified at Watkins Glen two weeks later, yet considered it an auspicious race. 'Watkins Glen was very important to us,' he told Elizabeth Hayward, 'because it was there that the car started to come good. It was there that we found the limit. It became a forgiving car. I had three pit stops for a sticking throttle, but being qualified second fastest I was sure we were going the right way with the car.' He had in fact been less than two-hundredths of a second slower in qualifying than pole-sitter and 1971 World Champion Jackie Stewart's Tyrrell.

'In many ways we started 1972 there,' said Emerson of the '71 American Grand Prix. With 16 points he ranked sixth in the 1971 World Championship. Adding Wisell's nine points placed Lotus fifth among constructors. These steady showings helped make up for the sad fact that this was the first year since 1959 in which Lotus failed to win a Formula 1 race of any description. The 72's improved form was underscored at Brands Hatch in October in a contest stopped after 15 laps when Jo Siffert crashed fatally. Emerson had set fastest lap and was lying second when the red flag waved.

Colin Chapman, Emerson and the team were starting to gel. Chapman, Fittipaldi told Gordon Kirby, 'was like a teacher or a tutor. Going through the problems you normally face with any Formula 1 car with Colin behind me was just fantastic. He could be very difficult sometimes but he knew a lot about motor racing and racing cars, more than anybody I ever worked with.' In 1971, he added, 'we spent one year developing the car and trying to work together well. I think when we started the next year everything worked, the whole organisation, with the right combination between the driver, the mechanics and the team manager.'

The Lotus boss returned the favour. 'There's no doubt that, at his best, Emerson was a fantastic driver,'

Chapman said. 'He was keen when he came to us, and demonstrated tremendous willingness to learn. We thrust him into the Grand Prix world pretty early, and he responded with that fantastic win at Watkins Glen. By 1972 he was right at the top, driving tremendously well.'

A striking Lotus change for 1972 was announced early in December of the previous year. Lotus backer Imperial Tobacco had revolutionised Formula 1 racing with its red and gold 'Gold Leaf' livery on the 1968 Lotuses. Now, launching its new 'John Player Special' cigarettes, it married racing car and pack design even more closely and indeed sensationally. Like the pack, the 72 carried the JPS logo in gold on a handsomely pin-striped glossy-black car that would also be known, appropriately but controversially, as the 'John Player Special.' It was a brilliant concept, good enough to be used as late as 1986.

'Lotus – sorry John Player Special – looked oppressively overdressed in their black and gold livery,' said *Motor* of the Argentine Grand Prix in January, 1972. 'The red flashes on the front of Emerson Fittipaldi's helmet looked quite frivolous in this setting while Dave Walker's white helmet looked downright disrespectful.' Like Fittipaldi the year before, Aussie Walker had won the Lombank Formula 3 championship in 1970. He was fated to do poorly in the senior category.

Counting again for points, the Argentine race found Fittipaldi challenging Stewart for the lead before retiring with suspension breakage. In South Africa Emerson led but was finally beaten by Denny Hulme's McLaren. Back in Britain in March in the Race of Champions at Brands, Fittipaldi's race was perfect: pole, fastest lap and victory. He managed everything but the fastest lap at Silverstone's non-championship race in April. Emerson was easily on pole and the leader of a small field in a non-points Formula 1 race at Interlagos at the end of March, paving the way for future championship contests there. A broken rear-suspension link retired him near the finish, disappointing his legions of home fans. Brother Wilson was third for Brabham.

'It is very important to go well at the beginning of the year,' Fittipaldi said of these races, 'because then everyone has high hopes. Everybody tries to work that little bit harder – the team, the mechanics, Colin, the tyre people.' Ralph Bellamy and Martin Wade were

Chapman's design team after the departure of Maurice Philippe. Preparation improved a lot, Emerson said: 'What Colin likes to do – and I think he is right – is to have a mechanic who takes care of each car. That way the mechanic who built the car at the beginning of the year always takes care of it. It is very important, because that mechanic knows all the details. If one day he has the same trouble he knows why, and how to cure the problem.'

Synthesis of driver, car and team was convincingly demonstrated in the Spanish Grand Prix with a brilliantly judged race in which Emerson had to protect his lead when a supplementary fuel tank sprang a leak. Fittipaldi changed his driving style to suit, using fewer revs to save fuel, and came home the winner. This, wrote Paul Sheldon, 'spoke volumes for the driving ability of the young Brazilian.' The only sour note was struck when the police on the podium guarding pretender to the throne Juan Carlos mistook an ebullient Colin Chapman for an attacking terrorist. He received an official apology for his torn coat.

'At Jarama on May Day,' echoed Michael Bowler in *Motor*, 'the John Player Special maintained its winning form in the hands of the young Brazilian. Once he had streaked past Stewart just beyond the pits on the ninth lap he never put a foot wrong. He pulled away from the opposition, only Jacky Ickx in a Ferrari finishing on the same lap as Fittipaldi. Jackie Stewart has tipped Emerson Fittipaldi as the man most likely to challenge his crown – and he is so right.'

Emerson went to Monaco equal in the standings to Denny Hulme and claimed pole with his Friday time. In a wet race he was third, picking up four useful points that put him clearly ahead of all rivals. Two weeks later he was in England's north-west at Oulton Park for a non-championship 110-mile race in which he was second to Hulme, hampered by an inappropriate choice of tyres. He won another non-points race at Vallelunga near Rome in June, particularly delighting Lotus's cigarette backers as the race was sponsored by rival Marlboro.

In 1971 Emerson's road accident had knocked him out of contention in mid-season. In 1972 it was Jackie Stewart's turn to be grounded, in his case by a stomach ulcer. Thus an on-form Fittipaldi was virtually unopposed in the Belgian Grand Prix at Nivelles. Nevertheless he had several factors on his side. One was increased support from the team for a clear contender for the world title. 'It helped me,' said Emerson. 'Everybody tried harder.' With this came increased respect for his technical contributions, as an example at Nivelles showed.

'At Nivelles,' said Emerson, 'I had a Formula 2 wing, from Brazil, on my Formula 1 car! I spoke to Colin and said, "I would like to try the Formula 2 wing, because I've had this experience in Formula 2. Moving it backward you have more effect and you can have less frontal area." He said, "What? Formula 2 wing on our Formula 1 car?" They didn't want to try it. I said, "Please, just take it along to try it." It was a yellow wing; they painted it black! We tried it at Nivelles, and I raced and I won with the Formula 2 wing!' Here, clearly, was a thinking driver which whom Warr and Chapman could make progress. 'Now Chapman and I get on well,' said Emerson. 'People always get on well when they're winning. Maybe things weren't so good at the beginning. But now they're okay!'

Another factor favouring Fittipaldi was good fortune, as Nivelles proved. 'The distributor cap wasn't fitted properly,' said Eddie Dennis, the Chief Mechanic, 'and all through the race it was gradually wearing away part of the contact points on the distributor. The car was running most of the race with the cap half off, and it is incredible that it could last that long.'

As the clear championship leader, young Fittipaldi found himself at the centre of unaccustomed attention. 'It's incredible how it changed,' he said. 'You feel a lot of pressure from everywhere. Before the race everybody says, "Oh, you have to win this race! You are leading the championship! After the race in Belgium, when I won, Jackie and I had dinner together. He said, "Emerson, you must be prepared now for the pressure because it is going to come from all over the world, people who want to do interviews and the people who ask: 'What do you think? Do you think you can win the championship?'" It is really amazing. Every day a different journalist is knocking at the front door of our house to ask what I think about this or that. Stewart was great with me. He taught me how to behave with regard to advertising contracts, relationships with fans and agreements with sponsors. He was a real friend!'

Anything but the stereotype fiery Latin, Fittipaldi had the calm centre he needed to survive the onslaught. His next race was on the 'mini-Nürburgring' of France's Clermont-Ferrand. Emerson admitted to Elizabeth Hayward that he hadn't come to terms with the track: 'Clermont is a good example of what happens when you have a short time to do everything together. I had never driven there before, so I didn't know the track well, and I couldn't give the right opinion on what to change.' Uncharacteristically he was almost five seconds off the sparkling pole time of Chris Amon's Matra and only a second or so quicker than his brother Wilson's Brabham. In the race he avoided the tyre problems that plagued others and finished second behind the recovered Stewart.

At Brands Hatch in July Fittipaldi was pipped for pole only by Jacky Ickx's Ferrari. In the race a close battle with Stewart was won by the Brazilian, who finished four seconds ahead. 'It had been a good race, often exciting and at all times interesting,' wrote Ray Hutton in *Autocar*, 'and Fittipaldi described it as the hardest he had ever driven in Formula 1. He leads the World Championship by 16 points. His performances become more and more impressive as the season goes on.'

Luck was on his side again in that British Grand Prix, said Eddie Dennis: 'He won the race and had a puncture on the slowing-down lap. When you have these sorts of lucky breaks, you know you're going to win, really.' Transaxle implosion scuppered a good effort in the German GP when Emerson was running second to eventual winner Ickx.

Emerson figuratively rubbed his hands at the thought of the next encounter on the Österreichring, a fast circuit much to his liking. Further encouragement came from a friend whom he called 'a fantastic person,' Edson Arantes do Nascimento, who sent Fittipaldi his football shirt. Better known as Pele, Brazil's soccer hero, he'd become – with the rest of Brazil – a Fittipaldi fan. Starting from pole, Emerson seized the lead from Stewart before half-distance and in what was called 'a dazzling display of flawless driving under pressure' held off Denny Hulme to win by 1.2 seconds at an average of 133.32mph for 198 miles. Instead of joining the others in the Morumbi room shared with Wilson, the Austrian Grand Prix trophy was sent to Pele.

Fittipaldi now had enough points to contemplate locking up the championship at the Italian Grand Prix four weeks later. As an intermezzo, however, he and Lotus entered the Rothmans 50,000 at Brands Hatch, named after its prize fund of £50,000, Europe's richest ever at the time. The race, over 312 miles, was open to all comers from Formula 1 to Can-Am. A brief flirtation with racing in the colours of Café do Brasil – a personal Fittipaldi sponsor – was abandoned when Imperial Tobacco saw a chance to tweak the nose of rival Rothmans.

Before the main event, its drivers contested a one-lap race in Ford tractors equipped with seat belts and rollover bars. From the front row Emerson took the lead, only to be caught by Tim Schenken, who shrewdly sped up by selecting neutral on a downhill section. Carlos Reutemann caught Fittipaldi by short-cutting across the infield so the Brazilian finished second with Schenken third. In the race proper Emerson 'made it look easy' in his Lotus 72 equipped with supplementary fuel and oil tanks, winning outright and collecting the £10,000 top prize.

At Monza in September the Grand Prix racers faced chicanes for the first time. This was the least of the difficulties encountered by Team Lotus, which in Emerson's words 'had problems all the time from Tuesday until a few seconds before the race,' which he started from the third row. By lap 17 of 55 he was running second behind the Ferrari of Jacky Ickx. Approaching the final ten laps he was husbanding his tyres 'because when I started to drive hard my tyres went off and I began to lose time,' in preparation for a challenge to Ickx, when the Belgian's red mount retired with a dead engine. Emerson had a clear lead.

Seeing the final chequer sparked no little emotion. 'As soon as I was level with the pits,' Fittipaldi told Elizabeth Hayward, 'I could see Colin jumping out over the guard-rail and throwing his hat in the air … and that was the happiest moment I have ever had in my racing career! It was just the right thing to happen – I couldn't believe it.' Emerson had seized the title by the throat, Ray Hutton reported: 'The Italian Grand Prix was another convincing win in an immensely successful season. Not for him the accumulation of championship points from mere placings; his victory at Monza was the fifth out of the ten championship rounds held so far.' 'Emerson really won that championship fairly and squarely,' seconded his chief mechanic Eddie Dennis.

In racing terms the rest of Fittipaldi's season was anticlimactic. 'I was very disappointed after the Italian Grand Prix,' he said. 'I had just become World Champion and didn't achieve anything in Canada and the United States.' In December, however, wrote Ray Hutton, 'Fittipaldi was seen doing some rather unusual lappery in the John Player Special at Nottingham. He was demonstrating the car to employees at John Player's new Horizon factory and did three laps of the building in the fog – including a spin when he lost his way!'

Like others in the racing world, Hutton was intrigued by news that leaked during August and September about the Lotus pairing for 1973. Thrusting Swede Ronnie Peterson was to replace the hapless Dave Walker. 'According to JPTL competitions manager Peter Warr,' wrote Hutton, 'the two drivers are to have "equal number one" status which means that they will have to provide two of everything – two spare cars, two sets of engines and two sets of mechanics. This sort of arrangement has never worked very well in the past for Lotus.'

Colin Chapman put a positive spin on the arrangement, which recalled the strong Clark/Hill pairing of 1967. 'Two drivers of the calibre of Emerson and Ronnie obviously have their own problems,' he said, 'and we'll just have to see how we get on. I think they're both very sensible drivers ... probably one of the few pairings that you can envisage which would get on harmoniously throughout the whole racing season and who realise that by pooling their resources and co-operating with each other they are in fact helping each other.'

In the event it worked well in one respect: Lotus became World Champion constructor, with 91 points to 82 for Tyrrell and 54 for McLaren. But the 'equal number one' concept saw Emerson second in the 1973 title race with 55 points, ahead of Peterson's 52. Both were trounced by Stewart in his final year with 71 points. The Brazilian started the season well, with wins in Argentina, Brazil and Spain, while the Swede was stronger in the second half, notching up four wins. According to Peter Warr the two drivers were allocated wins in their home races. Emerson collected his victory – to the rapt ecstasy of more than 100,000 of his countrymen – but Peterson, slowed by a deflating tyre, fell to second in Sweden behind Hulme.

Although the Fittipaldi–Peterson relationship in 1973 has gone down in history as troubled, Emerson hasn't seen it that way. He was aware of its risks, he said at the time: 'I have already told Ronnie it will be very difficult. There is a good understanding between myself and Ronnie; we don't want anyone to come between us. We have agreed this. If Ronnie has any problems he will talk to me, and if I have any I will talk to him. We will talk to nobody else.'

Although Ronnie outqualified Emerson by 11 races to 4, the results in racing terms were much more balanced. The Brazilian had five fastest laps to his credit against two for the Swede. In two events, Holland and Germany, Fittipaldi was hampered by ankle injuries from a Zandvoort practice crash. 'I enjoyed every minute of working with Ronnie,' Emerson told Gordon Kirby recently. 'Ronnie was a great team-mate. He was one of the best friends I ever had in racing. And, of course, we had some fantastic races together, really fantastic.' In 1974 they would again, albeit in different makes of cars.

A change to new-pattern Firestone tyres in 1971 upsets the 72's handling, which the team – distracted by work on a turbine-powered Lotus – finds difficult to fix. Qualifying second-fastest for the US Grand Prix in October 1971 (right and overleaf), Emerson credits improvements made there for the great success he achieves in 1972.

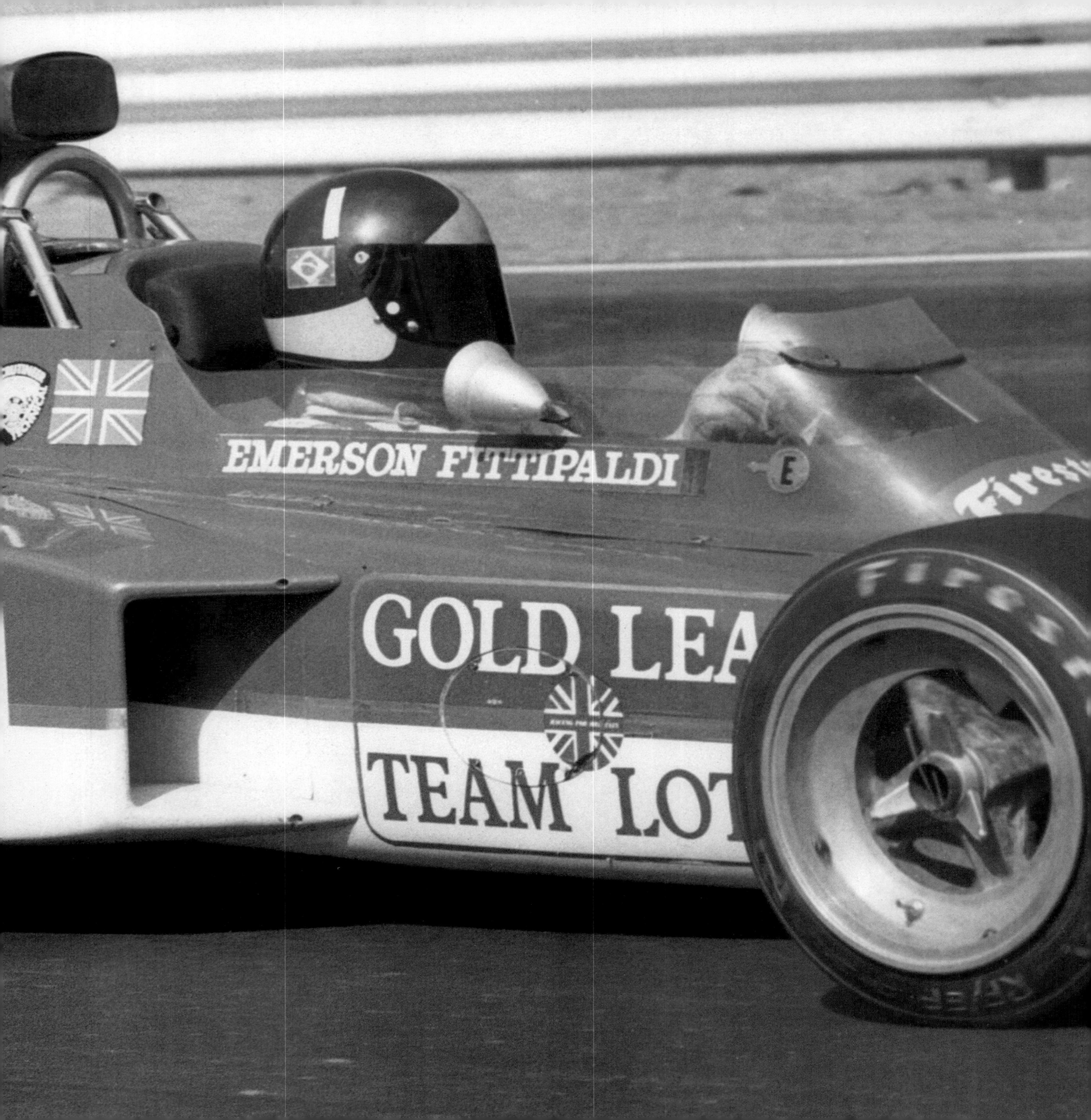
EMERSON FITTIPALDI
GOLD LEA
TEAM LOT
Firest
FIRES
E

The engaging, determined and obviously competent Fittipaldi forges an excellent working relationship with his crew at Team Lotus in the formative season of 1971. He regrets not having a better record at the demanding Nürburgring, where he qualifies eighth and retires in 1971 (preceding pages). He fails to finish at Watkins Glen (opposite) but his front-row grid position augurs well for 1972.

From a cantankerous beast at the beginning of 1971, Emerson develops the Lotus 72 into a car he calls the most forgiving he ever raced. On his way to the 1972 World Championship he wins from pole at Nivelles in Belgium (preceding pages), a feat he repeats in Austria. He compares notes with his brother Wilson (above), who competes in Formula 1 with the Brabham team in 1972 and '73.

Max Le Grand immortalises the instant that Fittipaldi crosses the finish line to win the British Grand Prix on 15 July 1972 (preceding pages). Fittipaldi is joined by his wife Maria Helena and Colin Chapman when the trophy is handed over by the RAC's Dean Delamont. At Brands not only the winner but also his car is paraded around the circuit to be lauded by the crowd. Emerson's look of quiet confidence is that of a true champion.

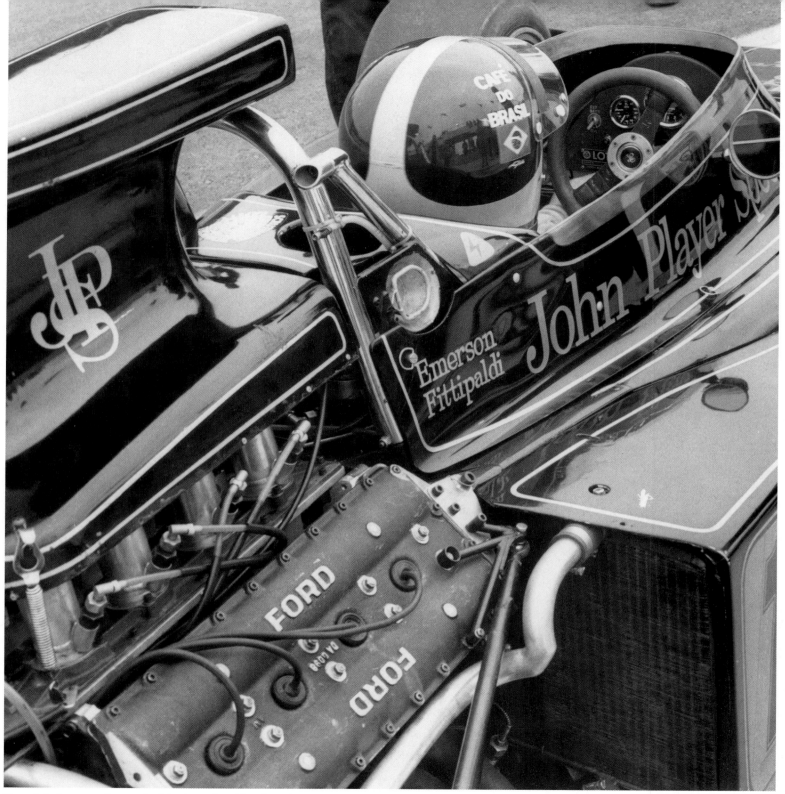

Exquisitely turned out, the black-and-gold John Player Special Lotus 72D sets a standard for style and elegance in Formula 1 racing cars that is seldom subsequently equalled. It is powered by the Cosworth-Ford V-8, the only engine that propelled Emerson Fittipaldi in more than a decade of Grand Prix racing. Having clinched the 1972 World Championship at Monza, Emerson regrets that his subsequent appearance in America (overleaf) falls short of success.

In Sweden in 1973 Fittipaldi is accompanied by his bearded manager Domingos Piedade, whose negotiating skills include fluency in half a dozen languages. Both Domingos and Colin Chapman are in high spirits as the reigning World Champion boards his paddock transport. Few drivers enjoy more popularity as champion than the likeable Brazilian.

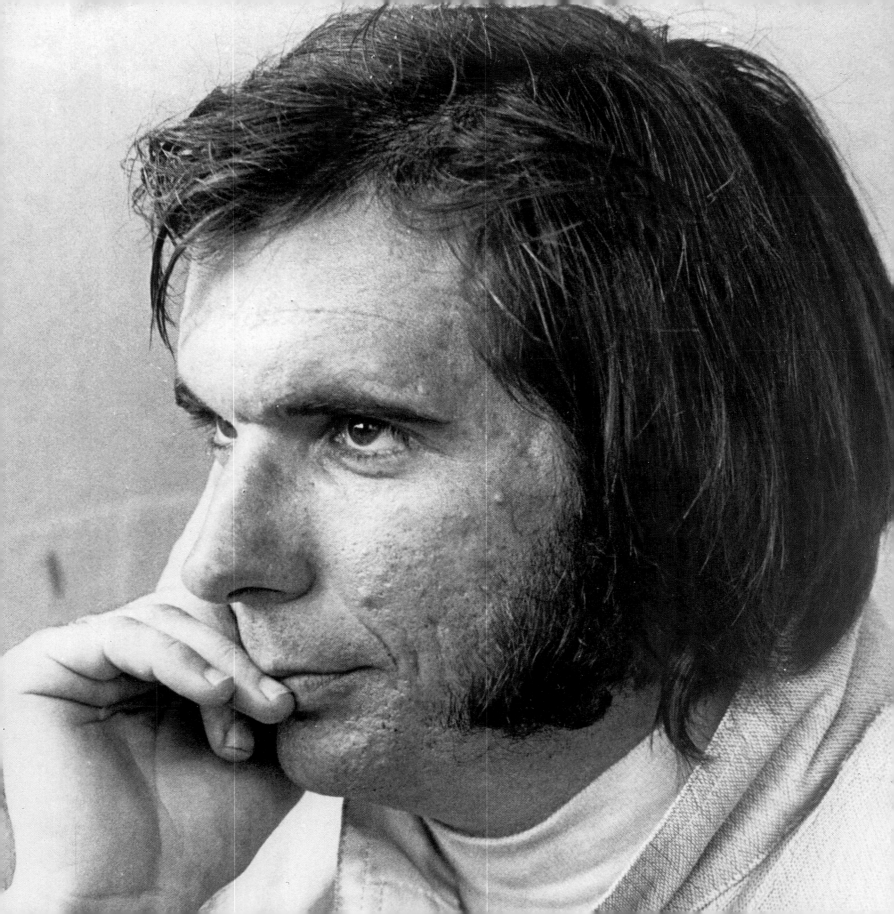

Emerson's personal sponsorship by Café do Brasil provokes controversy between himself and Colin Chapman, but as one of Brazil's most prominent global ambassadors his request to carry the decal could hardly be refused. His JPS-Lotus proudly flaunts the number 1 throughout the 1973 season, as Ove Nielsen depicts so strikingly (overleaf).

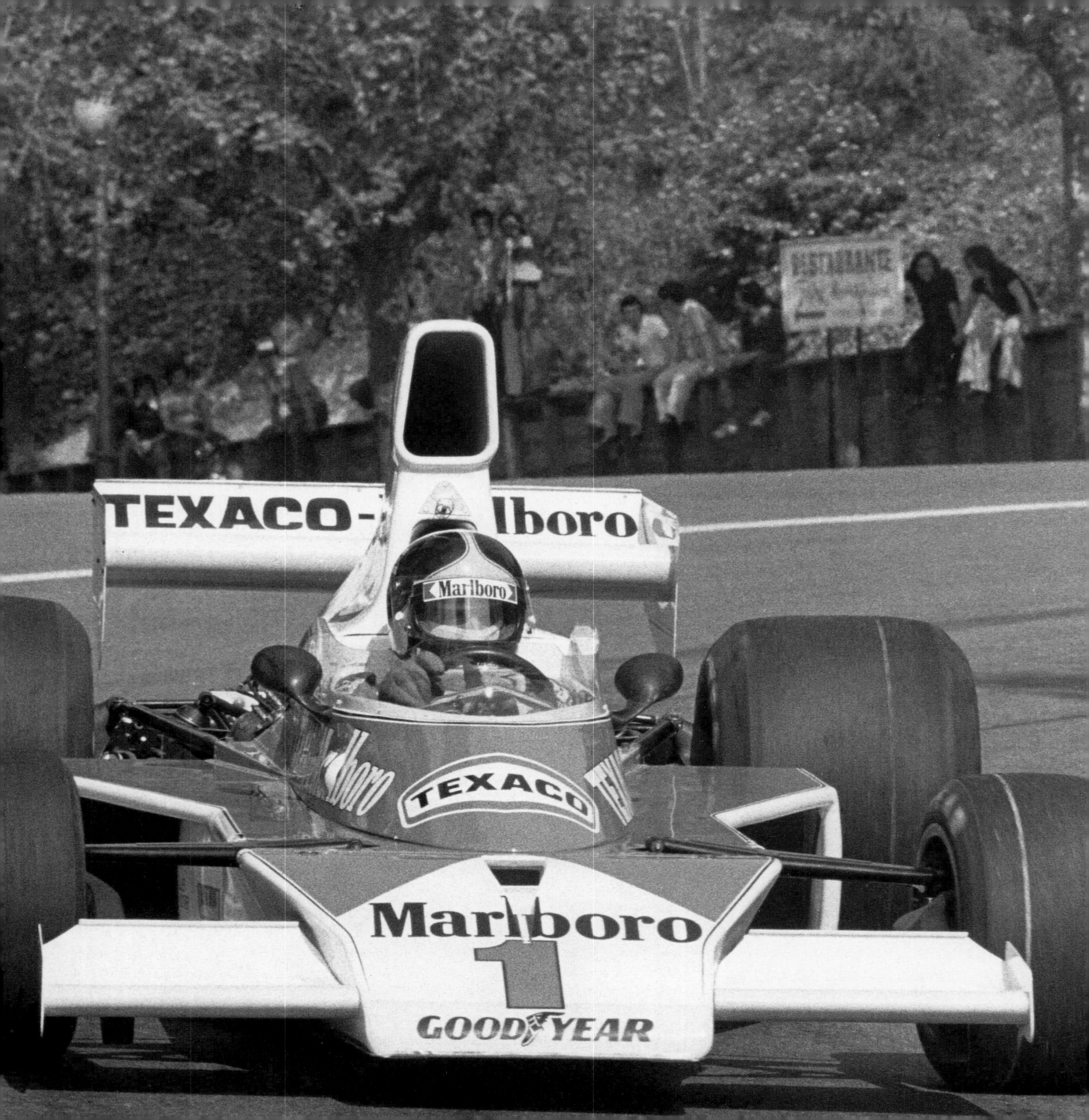
TEXACO-
lboro
Marlboro
TEXACO
Marlboro
1
GOODYEAR

CHAPTER 5

Marlboro Country

Nursing a 72 with a deflating right rear tyre, Emerson Fittipaldi won the Spanish GP on 29 April 1973 to give Lotus its historic 50th World Championship victory. 'Contingent of Brazilian fans including band from warship in Barcelona harbour go wild,' read a contemporary report. This was a full three years since the 72 had made its début in the Spanish race in 1970.

At the beginning of the '73 season in Argentina Emerson won what he called his greatest race to date, remorselessly grinding down the Tyrrells of Stewart and Cevert. 'For me it was the most fiercely competitive contest I have ever entered,' Fittipaldi said. 'A lot of other people want to have a crack at the champion and I was very much in the firing line when I prepared for this important race in Buenos Aires.'

With Chapman having to leave early, Peter Warr took charge of cap-throwing in Argentina. Afterward the tall,

Joint sponsorship by Marlboro and Texaco brings Emerson Fittipaldi to the McLaren team for the 1974 season. Many think the Brazilian mad to leave high-flying Lotus for McLaren, which has yet to win a championship, but by 1975 he is again wearing the coveted number 1 on his McLaren M23.

bespectacled team manager said, 'We were going to design a new car because we thought this one was getting a bit old-fashioned. Perhaps we don't need to after all.' Although said half in jest, this reflected the realities at Lotus. Colin Chapman had much else on his plate. He was closing Lotus Components after Mike Warner's departure, buying a boat company and investing in an all-new engine to power his production cars. In a spare moment Chapman did brief Ralph Bellamy to design a 'lighter 72,' work on which began during 1973.

No one knew better than Emerson the strengths and weaknesses of the 72. Once set up, he said, 'the Lotus 72 is very forgiving. And I know that well!' But setting it up was very demanding. In a meeting with Porsche engineers in October 1973, he told them that the 72 was perhaps still the best Formula 1 car, but that it had to be *very* precisely adjusted within narrow limits to give of its best: 'The Lotus 72 is a very difficult car to get on the limit. To get the right settings.' And he was good at getting them; Peterson's car often raced with Fittipaldi's settings after the Swede and his crew had lost their way.

Meanwhile McLaren had produced a new car, the M23, launched early in the 1973 season. Driven most successfully by Denny Hulme and Peter Revson, it scored three wins during the year. 'I had some of my toughest races in 1973 against the McLarens,' reflected Fittipaldi. He was impressed by the design from Gordon Coppuck's board; here, clearly, was a car with potential. But McLaren's sponsor, Yardley, was demanding more than the escalating costs of Formula 1 would allow McLaren to deliver. Into this fiscal gap stepped new parties with a successful Brazilian in tow.

'The first that we knew about it,' said McLaren chief Teddy Mayer, was that 'Marlboro and Texaco came to us and said, "We want to co-sponsor you, McLaren, and we want to bring Emerson as part of the package." We said "Fine!" We had a few arguments with Texaco over some technicalities but apart from that we were pretty happy with it. For those days it was good money. And we could run the team pretty sensibly.'

This grand alliance was the result of talks that the two sponsors held with Emerson in June and led to preliminary agreements with McLaren that were reached as early as July of 1973. The plans were kept under wraps. In fact the rumour mill had it that both Fittipaldi brothers would drive for Bernie Ecclestone's Brabham team in 1974. Emerson was supposed to be bringing Texaco sponsorship to Brabham, which Ecclestone acquired at the end of 1971. In fact this was a possibility until the McLaren opportunity opened up, as was a seat in a Tyrrell as well.

Fittipaldi was key to the new McLaren arrangements. He had come to know Texaco – and vice versa – with their backing of Lotus in 1973. Marlboro wanted to step up from its sponsorship of BRM to a team with a better chance of winning consistently, and a proven winner like Emerson was a virtual guarantee of success. This was not lost on Colin Chapman. 'He enjoyed having Emerson Fittipaldi in the team,' Hazel Chapman told Jabby Crombac. At the end of '73 Chapman offered what were described as 'handsome terms' to retain his services, but Fittipaldi's move to McLaren was a *fait accompli*.

'For me it was a very difficult decision, for sure,' Emerson told Gordon Kirby. 'Lotus was a great team and I felt very much at home there, like it was a family.' At the same time, however, he was unhappy about the division of resources that Chapman's 'dual Number One' policy created: 'The team's efforts are concentrated neither on Ronnie nor on me, but are divided in two.' The new alignment promised better results: 'Marlboro is a huge company and there was no doubt in my mind that they were very serious about winning Grand Prix races. And, of course, McLaren had been very competitive in Formula 1. Finally, I decided it was the way to go.' Having just turned 27, Fittipaldi still had much to offer.

Over the 1974–75 winter he plunged into development work with his new team, doing all the testing of Coppuck's M23 improvements at Paul Ricard while teammate Hulme wintered in New Zealand. 'I liked him straight away,' said Teddy Mayer, 'because he was very reliable from the point of view of not damaging your car – he only spun once in the whole time he drove for us. But apart from that his information was excellent. He was very clear on what his response was to what you'd done to the car and when he needed to go fast he seemed to be able to do it. So we thought that was great.'

His first impression of the M23 was positive. 'It's a very, very conventional car, built very simply,' said Emerson. 'It's a car that's easy to make handle well on any circuit in the world because it's so simple. The basic suspension settings are sound. It's very, very quick, perhaps the quickest of all the cars, on fast corners. And it's a very forgiving car to drive. You can keep it on the limit all the time.' Above all he praised the package, the team that Teddy Mayer and Phil Kerr had rescued from the death of its founder only four years earlier. 'Now I can say I am certainly with the best team in Formula 1,' said Fittipaldi. 'Perhaps the car is not the best – I can't say for sure – but the *team* is fantastic.'

He showed his enthusiasm at the new season's first race in Argentina, wrote Doug Nye: 'In the Buenos Aires paddock the Brazilian 1972 World Champion bubbled with unmitigated delight at his new team and car. He covered more practice laps than anyone else – 97 – and hurled the new M23 round with controlled forcefulness.' However, Emerson's début for his new team was embarrassing. From third on the grid he ran third for the first three laps, only to have a plug lead come adrift, requiring a pit stop. Back in the race, he inadvertently hit a steering-wheel-mounted switch that cut the ignition. He'd unbuckled himself when he discovered why the engine had stopped, so he had to pit again to have his straps done up. Fittipaldi finished 10th, two laps back, while his Kiwi team-mate won.

In front of his rabid fans at Interlagos Emerson was on coruscating form, placing top in three of the four practice sessions and starting from pole. He was in the lead when the race was stopped on the 32nd of its 40 laps after a tropical rainstorm. On the following weekend a 136-mile race was run on a new circuit at Brasilia, Brazil's capital, for which a dozen cars were brought inland from Sao Paulo. In a virtual command performance, Emerson took pole, fastest lap and the victory.

The non-championship races at Brands and Silverstone, judged so important by Emerson to give momentum to a new season, failed to produce for him in 1974. He was third at a rain-swept Brands Hatch in March and in April missed the Silverstone race to attend to an illness in his family. Between them was the last 'away' race at South Africa's Kyalami circuit. Plagued by harsh vibrations from their Goodyears, the McLarens placed seventh (Fittipaldi) and ninth (Hulme). Reutemann won, and in Spain the victory went to Niki Lauda, so the first four races of '74 had four different winners. With as many as 60 cars eligible to race and some contests starting with more than 30 on the grid, it was bidding to be a hyper-competitive year.

From Spain, where Fittipaldi finished third, his season started looking up. The Belgian GP in May was again on the 2.3-mile circuit at Nivelles, which the cars lapped in little more than 70 seconds. Fittipaldi was part of a leading clump of cars until they started lapping the tail-enders, when he slipped by Clay Regazzoni's Ferrari into the lead. Hard on his tail was the other Ferrari driven by Niki Lauda, but Emerson held on to win with a margin of just a third of a second over the Austrian.

'Emerson's drive at Nivelles was very outstanding,' recalled McLaren's Teddy Mayer. 'Emerson was sensible, clever and, above all, experienced. He would think out his strategy in a race, always running as gently as he dared to get a good result. He could be very quick but was always very tidy and he always kept his head. He spent a lot of time thinking about it. He was always fit, kept himself fit, worked at it very hard.' Emerson returned the compliment: 'Teddy is dedicated one

hundred per cent to the team. He lives and works for the McLaren team, which for me is fantastic.'

Fit or not, Fittipaldi was less than his effervescent self at Monaco at the end of May. He and Denny were both mid-grid with identical times. While his team-mate crashed out on the first lap and took five cars with him, Emerson snuck by to settle into fifth place. Too far from fourth, he was concentrating on keeping John Watson's Brabham behind him and seemed settled at a comfortable gait. It was an example of a philosophy about which the Brazilian was open: 'There are many races and it's not worth taking a risk to win one at all costs. Sometimes I've given up on winning so as not to face a pointless risk.' When he was lapped by Ronnie Peterson's leading Lotus 72, however, Fittipaldi picked up the pace. Being upstaged by his erstwhile team-mate wasn't to his liking.

Emerson's fifth place at Monaco was followed by fourth in Sweden. Married with his two wins these gave him a five-point championship lead, but he was chased hard by the Ferraris of Regazzoni and Lauda, and the Tyrrell of South African Jody Scheckter. His lead narrowed after the Dutch GP at Zandvoort, where he was third behind the two Ferraris. And it vanished after the French race at Dijon, where he was running fourth when his engine expired – his first retirement of the year.

Starting with its problems in South Africa, McLaren struggled with Goodyear's latest tyres in the early part of the season. 'Their new tyres,' said Fittipaldi, 'were smaller in diameter, wider and more rigid, not well suited to our car.' Gordon Coppuck made significant changes to the M23's suspension to accommodate them. A test session at Silverstone evaluated the result in July. After the test, said Teddy Mayer, 'I remember Emerson saying to me, "Now I can go and win the championship."'

The new suspension's first test was in the British GP at Brands in July. Fittipaldi was eighth on the grid, albeit only 0.8 second slower than pole. Rivals' pit stops helped him rebound to second at the finish behind Scheckter, reviving his championship hopes. These dipped again after the German GP at the Nürburgring, a circuit which Emerson had always itched to conquer. This time he came to his third place on the grid after last-minute efforts to get his engine to run properly and faltered at the start, failing to find first gear. He was hit from behind by none other than team-mate Hulme.

'They touched,' Ray Hutton reported, 'with such force that a rear upright on Hulme's car was broken and Fittipaldi's rear suspension was slightly damaged. The Brazilian did less than half a lap before it was reported that he had a puncture at that same left rear wheel. The McLarens, like the Brabhams, were carrying canisters of pressurised tyre sealant as a "get you home" measure but Fittipaldi found that the hole in his tyre was too big for such treatment and crawled back to the pits in first gear on the flat.' He completed three laps before retiring with transmission problems.

Austria as usual was much to Emerson's liking. On the grid in Austria he was headed only by Reutemann's Brabham and Lauda's Ferrari. He followed these two in the race as well but had to retire on lap 37 of the 54 with a duff engine. From a clear championship lead at mid-season Fittipaldi was now well in arrears with 37 points to 41 for Scheckter and 45 for Regazzoni. This bitterly competitive season had already seen seven different drivers win Grands Prix. Picking a likely champion was anything but easy.

Unlike 1972, Emerson had no chance of wrapping up a title at Monza in September. His best hope from sixth on the grid was a podium finish. The two Ferraris that started ahead of him obliged by breaking their flat-12 engines, leaving the Brazilian in a close battle with his 1973 team-mate's Lotus 72. A challenge at one of the chicanes failed to come off and Fittipaldi finished second behind Ronnie Peterson. The gap was 0.8 second, exactly the same as it had been the previous year – and in the same order – when both were driving Lotuses.

With Scheckter also gaining points for third, Monza tightened the title race. The two North American contests remained. The first was at Mosport in Canada, not far from Toronto. McLaren tried to even the odds for this one by air-freighting a spare M23 from Monza for testing on the bumpy and hilly circuit, but rain put a stop to anything but testing for wet-weather conditions.

On the race weekend Fittipaldi's determination was plain to see, wrote Doug Nye: 'Emerson was holding nothing back and made his bid for the championship in practice with a spectacular drive showing all his old skill and commitment to qualify on pole.' His front-row partner was Niki Lauda, who charged into an immediate lead ahead of Emerson. Behind him were title rivals Scheckter – who retired – and Regazzoni, who placed second when Fittipaldi moved to first after Lauda hit some wreckage and spun off. 'If Niki didn't spin, for sure he was going to win,' said the fortunate victor.

Now Fittipaldi and Regazzoni were tied on 52 gross points with one race to go. Both had enough pointless finishes that neither would be required by the rules to shed points at season's end. It was all up to 59 laps and 200 miles at Watkins Glen.

Emerson was eighth on the grid, behind rival Jody Scheckter and ahead of Clay Regazzoni, who was struggling with his Ferrari's handling. Neither figured in the race, the South African retiring and the Swiss pitting for a change of tyres. Fittipaldi held fourth for the final laps. 'Fittipaldi ran a careful race,' wrote F. David Stone. 'Fourth place was enough to make sure that he won the championship fair and square, without recourse to the tie-deciders that would have been necessary had the season ended with two drivers on the same number of points. It was a fine and fair conclusion to one of the best years of Grand Prix racing in memory.'

The result was historic for McLaren, which had entered Formula 1 in 1966. This was its first drivers' championship. Thanks to 20 points from Denny Hulme – who quit racing after the Glen – McLaren also collected the makes title. 'I was very proud to be the first World Champion with Marlboro,' Emerson said. 'Again, I was in the right place at the right time, with the right people. It was a great experience. Those were the top memories.' In some circles there was surprise as well, after Fittipaldi left high-flying Lotus for struggling McLaren. 'When Emerson – having won the championship – decided to drive for McLaren, everybody thought the man is crazy!' recalled top mechanic Jo Ramirez. 'And he provided McLaren with another championship!'

Fittipaldi fitted some other driving commitments into his 1974 schedule. In July he returned to karting for an event organised by sponsor Marlboro at an English track. 'It took Emerson less than half a lap of the bumpy little circuit to get used to 20bhp and 100cc again and to start setting competitive times,' Ray Hutton reported.

With Ferrari finally extracting the best from its 312T and the skills of Niki Lauda, 1975 was the Austrian's year. He won five of the 14 races and the championship with 64.5 points. Emerson was vice-champion with two wins – Argentina and Britain – four second places and 45 points. The season was 'definitely tougher', said McLaren's Mayer, with Ferrari making 'quite a bit of improvement in their engine and a little bit in their car.' Nevertheless, he added, 'It wasn't a disaster at all. At times he got a little bit distracted with his brother's ill-fated Formula 1 project.'

Fittipaldi started the season in storming style at Buenos Aires. 'Anybody who had doubts about Emerson Fittipaldi being crowned the 1974 World Champion would have seen just how he earned that crown,' wrote Geoff Hutchinson in *Autocar*, 'when he scored the first win of the new season at last Sunday's Argentine Grand Prix. In front of a capacity 180,000-strong crowd, chanting for its countryman Carlos Reutemann since the early hours of the morning, Fittipaldi drove a cool race under the blazing sun to take the flag just 5.9 seconds clear of James Hunt's Hesketh, and 17 seconds ahead of Reutemann's Martini-Brabham.' Hunt was leading until he spun under intense pressure from the Brazilian.

The race Emerson really wanted was a fortnight later at Interlagos, where he qualified on the front row but made a dismal start, falling to seventh on the first lap. He battled back into contention to finish second behind fellow countryman Carlos Pace's Brabham under 400,000 ecstatic Brazilian eyes. 'For the last eight laps,' wrote Hutchinson, 'Fittipaldi pulled out all the stops, and when the chequered flag came out, the two Brazilians were only 5.8 seconds apart. It sent the crowd into delighted chanting and flag-waving for their two national heroes.'

South Africa, where Emerson was running fourth when a loose distributor wire dropped him from contention, was best forgotten. Neither were the two non-points races in Britain very bracing, with a fifth at Brands and a second at Silverstone, the latter only a tenth of a second behind winner Lauda. Fittipaldi was struggling with the handling of McLaren's revised M23, as designer Gordon Coppuck admitted: 'At the beginning of the season we had a lot of understeer in the car. We tried a new front and rear suspension together to get rid of our understeer and ended up with oversteer.'

In the wet at Monaco, with drivers changing to dry tyres at one-third distance, Emerson seized a welcome second place. This momentum was dissipated at Zolder and Andersdorp, where Fittipaldi finished just out of the points. Holland was another wet race but Emerson couldn't exploit it, retiring with a fatigued engine. At Paul Ricard for the French GP it was new team-mate Jochen Mass's turn to carry the mail for McLaren, qualifying ahead of Fittipaldi and placing third ahead of the Brazilian's fourth place.

Before Silverstone in July McLaren's Gordon Coppuck said he'd 'been concentrating on making the car more neutral, and as it now seems suited to medium to high speed corners, we've got every reason to feel optimistic.' This was the ticket for the fast Northamptonshire track, where Emerson started from the fourth row of a rain-squalled race. On the 56th of 67 laps 'the cars came, at Stowe, upon a huge shower of rain,' wrote Paul Sheldon. 'The clever Fittipaldi got through the chaos but almost everyone else went off.' Emerson was declared the winner, 'being the only driver to keep full control in the appalling circumstances.' 'It really was a flash of the old Fittipaldi,' wrote Alan Henry in *Motoring News*. 'Emerson had kept his head and control while all around were losing theirs. It was a mark of his class.'

Although Emerson was eighth fastest on the grid for the German GP, by dint of devilish driving Jochen Mass was 0.9 second and two places farther forward for his home event. He crashed out of the first lap while Fittipaldi managed two more before retiring with suspension damage. Qualifying third fastest at one of his favourite tracks, the Österreichring, Emerson was badly placed this time when the race was called off on account of rain near half-distance and he finished out of the points.

'Toward the end of the summer,' Doug Nye wrote, 'people close to Fittipaldi were talking of his having decided to retire from racing. But by the time of the Italian GP at Monza he'd changed his mind. And it showed, as he drove in magnificent style there.' At Monza in September Regazzoni's win and Lauda's third sealed the latter's championship and a banner year for Ferrari. 'Fittipaldi,' wrote Geoffrey Williams, 'while not exactly extinguishing Ferrari celebrations, certainly put a damper on them.' From third on the grid he challenged the red cars and split them seven laps from the end to finish second. Nineteen seventy-five's final race was at Watkins Glen, where Emerson and the M23 were on awesome form. They were on the front row of the grid next to pole man Lauda, whom they followed doggedly from flag to flag. Fittipaldi set the fastest lap on his determined drive to second, five seconds behind Lauda.

At every race of 1975 the attending journalists voted for the best performances, regardless of finishing places. The overall winner for the season of the Prix Rouge et Blanc Josef Siffert was Emerson Fittipaldi. He was lifted into the lead by what was called 'his fiery drive' in the American Grand Prix. He took the honour for 1975 ahead of James Hunt, Jochen Mass and Vittorio Brambilla.

Fittipaldi-McLaren still looked a good partnership. A new M26 was said to be on the way, with a six-speed gearbox. 'Emerson Fittipaldi will be staying with Marlboro team Texaco in 1976,' wrote Peter Windsor in July, 1975, 'and will even be renewing his contract with McLaren on 1 August.' But he didn't. And he didn't. 'He was clearly interested in his brother's project,' said Teddy Mayer, 'the Brazilian Formula 1 car. I think if we could have afforded to pay him what he wanted he probably would have stayed, but Philip Morris didn't want to up the ante that much. The increase they offered him was about one-third or more.'

This didn't match the appeal of an even better pay packet to drive the Fittipaldis' very own car. 'Towards the end of 1975,' wrote Doug Nye, 'Emerson Fittipaldi's third-year McLaren contract option should have been exercised, but he delayed signing. Testing at Ricard in November '75 he crashed and broke a finger after setting the fastest time amongst the teams running there. At Colnbrook Teddy Mayer had been trying to finalise Emerson's signature for another season, with a deadline of November 25. Then at 8pm on Saturday, November 22 the phone rang in his home in Esher. It was the Brazilian double World Champion, calling from a coin box at Zurich airport. 'I've called to tell you I'm not going to sign. I've signed with my brother Wilson for our own team next year.'

Mayer, the story goes, was less than cordial on his end of the line. 'Poor Teddy,' said Fittipaldi. 'I think he was desperate. But he can't complain. After all, it was me who brought the sponsorship of Marlboro and Texaco to the team. And his contract with the sponsors will not expire before the next three years.' McLaren bounced back with its engagement of James Hunt, winning another world title in 1976.

'Working with the McLaren team and Teddy Mayer was really something,' Fittipaldi summed up, 'because that was a great team. The M23 was a really quick car and we were very competitive in 1974. There were a lot of good relationships and good teamwork at McLaren. I enjoyed it a lot and it was a great experience. When I look back on it, I realise that leaving Marlboro and McLaren was one of the biggest mistakes I ever made in my life.'

Having raced against the then-new McLaren M23 in 1973, Fittipaldi has high respect for its capabilities. He opens his 1974 account with a sensational victory at Interlagos (overleaf), starting from pole and winning after prevailing in a battle with his 1973 Lotus team-mate, Ronnie Peterson (1).

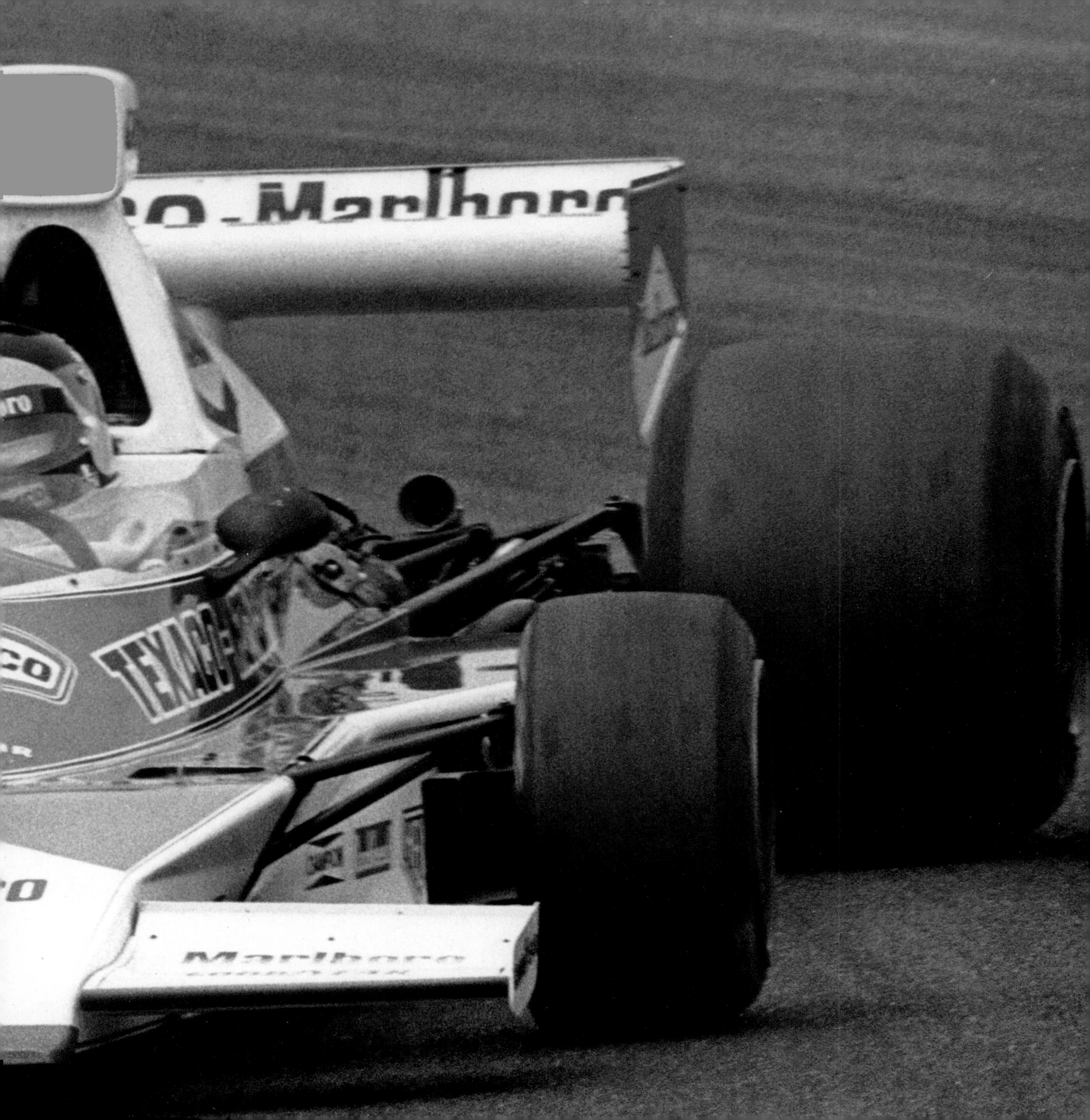
TEXACO
Marlboro

Strong financial backing helps the McLaren team to test extensively in 1974, test driving being a Fittipaldi strength. Only after the M23's roll centres are changed in a Silverstone test does Emerson feel he has a car he could race to the championship.
He drives the McLaren to its limits (preceding pages) against all rivals including the sister M23 entered by McLaren with Yardley sponsorship for Mike Hailwood (overleaf).

Fittipaldi makes no secret of his desire to use the best safety equipment available. His helmet is equipped with a fresh-air system to help him breathe in the event of a fire, and a physician accompanies him to all races. Prudent though his preparations are, they aren't needed by a driver who becomes legendary for his accident-free racing.

At Watkins Glen in 1970 the youthful-looking Fittipaldi (opposite with his wife Maria Helena) is a surprise winner at the age of 23. He is back again a year later as a known quantity (top left). The Fittipaldi physiognomy matures during his decade in Grand Prix racing.

Pole position for the Race of Champions at Brands Hatch means champagne for Fittipaldi and his crew; Emerson enjoys a glass in his cockpit. He goes on to win the 1972 race in his JPS-Lotus.

A portfolio of Emerson's mounts from his Formula 1 years shows him in the Dutch Grand Prix of 1975 (top) where his M23 McLaren retires, at Watkins Glen in his Lotus 72 where he is delayed by pit stops in 1971 (middle) and at Monaco in 1980 where he finishes just in the points in his Fittipaldi F7.

Emerson's CART-series transport includes the Penske-Chevrolet he drives to victory at Indy in 1993 (top), the Lola T87-Chevrolet with which he competes at Laguna Seca in 1988 (middle) and the spectacular Penske-Mercedes in which he suffers a career-ending crash in Michigan in 1996 (bottom). In his Patrick-entered March-Chevy he races Michael Andretti at Phoenix in April 1988 (overleaf).

In a span of two decades, from the JPS-Lotus of the early 1970s to the Penskes of the early 1990s, the distinctive helmet style of Emerson Fittipaldi remains the same in its colours but differs in design. Both are the mark of a wily and relentless competitor.

Compelled by the high expectations of their countrymen, Emerson and his brother Wilson expend all their energies and much of their fortune on building and racing their own Grand Prix cars from 1975 to 1982. In 1976 Emerson picks up a point for a sixth-place finish in the Monaco Grand Prix (opposite).

Emerson starts 1990, his first season for the Penske team, as reigning CART champion with a fifth-place finish on the Phoenix one-mile oval. He is competitive in 1991 with his Penske PC20-Chevrolet on the Long Beach street circuit (opposite).

The years are different but the concentration is the same. Fittipaldi checks his M23 environment in 1975 (opposite) and in 1974, the year in which he brings McLaren its first-ever World Championship.

Although not known for a spectacular driving style, Fittipaldi presses on with visible aggression at both Sweden (opposite, above) and Holland (opposite, below) during the 1975 season in his vain chase of Niki Lauda's Ferrari. His fast company in the Swedish race (above) includes McLaren team-mate Jochen Mass.

The many faces of Emerson, as pictured in his two McLaren years by Ove Nielsen, range from the sleepy to the sceptical and from the pleased to the perplexed. Above all he is an inquisitive racer who never stops learning from experiences both good and bad.

The McLaren M23 is nose-down under braking at Zandvoort (preceding pages). Emerson checks lap times with Maria Helena and logistics with a McLaren crew member in 1975. In Holland in 1975 he makes his point to a sceptical Teddy Mayer (opposite).

Ford-powered all, Fittipaldi is ahead of Jean-Pierre Jarier's Shadow and chasing team-mate Jochen Mass and countryman Carlos Pace's Brabham at Zandvoort in 1975 (opposite, above and overleaf). The Dutch race is won by James Hunt, who replaces Emerson at McLaren the following season.

Emerson joins Jackie Stewart as a proponent of stylish sunglasses on the Grand Prix circuit. Ample layers of Nomex are tugged on in preparation for a race in 1974 that will take Fittipaldi to the world title. Designed by Gordon Coppuck, his McLaren M23 (overleaf) is a well-balanced machine that benefits from Emerson's valuable testing input.

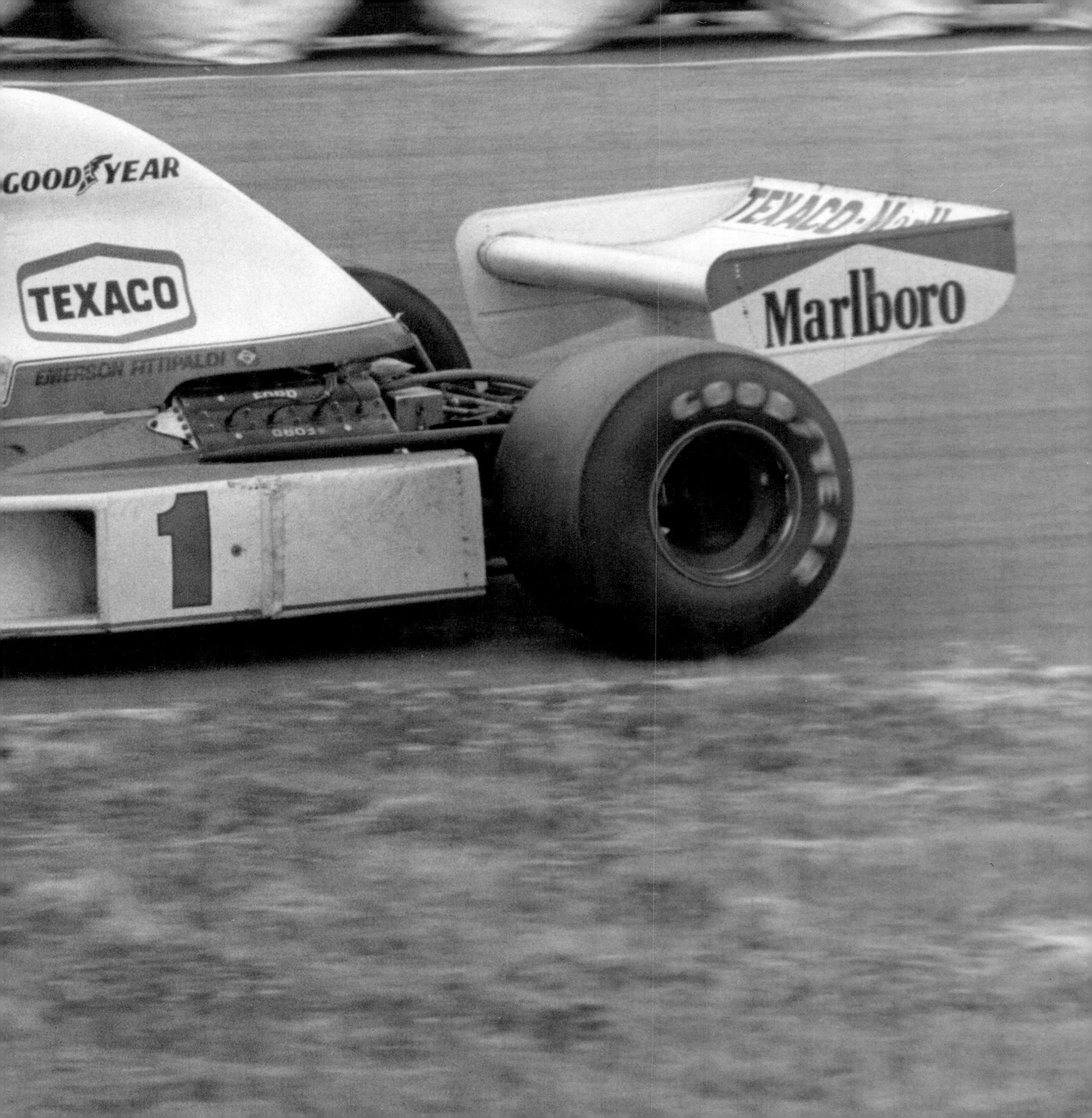
GOODYEAR
TEXACO
EMERSON FITTIPALDI
Marlboro
1

CHAPTER 6

Bittersweet Seasons

Emerson couldn't help being distracted. With his usual concentration he was chasing Lauda's Ferrari hard in a dispute over fourth place in the early laps of the Argentine Grand Prix. McLaren's reigning World Champion, he was eager to start the 1975 season as he meant to continue. But on the 13th lap – 'I hate number 13' – a pillar of black smoke billowed from a wrecked competitor. It was number 30, a glint of its silver paint just visible. It was the new car of his brother Wilson, the first-ever Fittipaldi Formula 1 car, in its baptismal race.

Emerson's concern over his brother's welfare was obvious from the Buenos Aires pits. But it was quickly confirmed that Wilson was – amazingly – unharmed by the crash, triggered by a broken half-shaft, that hurled his racer against the guard rails and brought massive fire trucks to the scene. Reassured by signs from his pit,

Very much the modern gladiator in his AGV crash helmet, Emerson Fittipaldi carries the bright colours of the Sao Paulo state sugar co-operative Copersucar into a new era of racing cars built by his own organisation. The project exacts a heavy toll both psychologically and financially.

Emerson lit the fire under his own attack. When Reutemann faltered Hunt took the lead, only to be pressured into a mistake by the red and white McLaren on his tail. Emerson started the '75 season with a convincing win. But his brother's car – the focus of their mutual hopes and desires – was a smouldering wreck.

It would take more than a disaster of this magnitude to discourage the car-mad Fittipaldi brothers from pursuing their dream of a Grand Prix machine from their own workshops. In 1972 Emerson said, 'I'd like to build a racing car with my brother Wilson. I've got a few good ideas.' A year later he demurred when asked about it by Mary Schnall Heglar: 'Mmmm, I don't think so,' he said, 'but his eyes were twinkling unduly, I thought,' the author added. 'I want to concentrate still for many years on driving,' Emerson explained, 'because when you start building, you cannot concentrate on driving. And I don't want to build while I can still be a driver.'

Such resolution wilted in the face of his brother's enthusiasm: 'I said to Emerson, "Why don't we build a Formula 1?" and then I put my fingers in my ears because I was sure he would say that I was crazy, but he only answered, "Yes, why don't we?"' That's how Wilson

Fittipaldi Jnr. described the conversation in September 1973 that led to the creation of the first-ever Brazilian Grand Prix car.

In the autumn of 1973 the brothers decided that Wilson would take a year off from racing to build it. By the end of the year they'd set up shop in the two-storey building across the street from the Interlagos track, south-west of Sao Paulo, where they'd built many of their early cars and based a driving school. Their first car was complete as a rolling chassis in September, 1974. It was publicly shown in Brasilia, the nation's capital, in October, and was track-tested for the first time at Interlagos on Monday, 18 November. Its fiery début was on the following 12th of January.

To create their car the Fittipaldis had been home-growing a talented designer, Richard Divila. Before his stint as mechanic to the Fittipaldi Formula 2 team in Europe in 1970, aeronautically trained Divila had extensively tunnel-tested a scale model of a planned Alfa-powered sports-racer. By the time Wilson tapped him to design their racer, Divila had gathered valuable know-how as a mechanic and then as a team manager in both Formula 2 and F1.

In support was Yoshiatsu Itoh, formerly with Lotus, in charge of construction and crew chief thereafter. General manager was Thomas Hardtmeier, brother of Wilson's charming wife Suzy. Team manager was Joaquin 'Jo' Ramirez, a Mexican who joined the group after more than five years of wrench-wielding for Dan Gurney, two for John Wyer and two for Ken Tyrrell. His hiring was Emerson's idea, Ramirez recalled: 'Emerson thought that it was a very good idea for Wilson to have someone Latin who had the same kind of mentality and could speak the languages, and that's how they offered me the job.

'The times were really very, very hard,' Jo reflected. 'You can imagine trying to make a Formula 1 car in Brazil – and they wanted it to be done in Brazil. The Brazilians are very nationalistic and that was a dream that they had. It was a desire to do something in the country so that Brazil would feel more involved in the sport. The Fittipaldis created a name in Brazil for motor-sport, so the next thing was to do their own cars.'

Getting needed materials was a daunting challenge, Ramirez recalled: 'Everything had to come from England

or the States or Europe; materials like steel, aluminium, rubber bags for the fuel tanks, brakes. Even with a name like Fittipaldi, which was quite famous, it was so difficult. Bits and pieces would be in customs for months and months. Wilson was very forceful and of course he knew the right people to help us to get the stuff in, but it was always hard.' And when Wilson called on Brazilian officials to get a carnet to ease his specially equipped Mercedes-Benz van through Europe's customs barriers, he was told that it was the first such request in the nation's history!

Wilson and Emerson launched the project from their pooled finances. Their title sponsor was Copersucar, a Sao Paulo state co-operative of sugar and alcohol producers headed by Jorge Volney Atalla with the experienced Paulo Nascimento as his marketing director. They saw every chance of an enhanced reputation in their support of the Fittipaldi venture. Copersucar's multicoloured avian motif was painted on a car whose base colour was silver. Why silver, once the hallowed hue of German racers? 'Because nobody else is using it!' said an unrepentant Emerson.

With Divila's original design, low-profile and adventurously aerodynamic, Wilson failed to qualify for two races and could finish no better than 10th, and that in the 1975 season's last race in America. For 1976, however, the team took three steps forward. One was a move to Britain. 'We set up a base in Caversham near Reading,' said Ramirez, 'a very small base. Then we moved to Slough and that was much larger, much more expensive. It was hard to pay for that, but it was a lot better.' A second step was its design and build of what Divila called "a more conventional kit car," still Ford-Cosworth-powered. Emerson oversaw its details and even tested it clandestinely, wearing an anonymous white helmet. 'He quite liked it,' Divila recalled. The new team's third step was the engagement of indisputably one of the leading drivers of the day, Emerson Fittipaldi.

One issue had to be resolved before Emerson could join the team. What would Wilson do? He asked his brother. 'I would quit,' came Wilson's ready reply. They had their eyes on blond Ingo Hoffman, a promising Paulista, as a second driver. Key discussions between Emerson and Copersucar were held between 11 November and the

21st, the date on which he signed a contract to drive for the family team in 1976.

It was the smallest Formula 1 car at the beginning of the season,' Emerson said of his new FD04. 'It had a very short wheelbase and tracks that were narrow in front and average in the rear. Very conventional, the Copersucar was simple and quite heavy – but not so much as to have affected the performance. It was a very sensitive car, responsive to changes, but it was never very forgiving and it was never very good under braking.'

The first test for the new combination came in the hothouse atmosphere of Brazil's Interlagos on 25 January. Pre-race testing was hugely promising. 'When we went to Brazil for the pre-tests for the Grand Prix,' said Jo Ramirez, 'Emerson did the fastest time ever there. He was going very quickly and we were really very pleased with the car. Everything was fine.' 'By 50 per cent luck and 50 per cent judgement,' Divila recalled, 'we had a car that was set up for Interlagos. We were as fast as the Ferraris.'

During qualifying, however, problems cropped up with the driver, not the car. Emerson pulled a shoulder muscle in a tennis match. 'He couldn't drive more than three, four laps at a time,' said Ramirez. 'He was really in agony. He qualified fifth, which was still fantastic, but he couldn't repeat the times that would have put him on a par with the time we did earlier. And then at the start of the race, in the first few laps, he had a problem with his spark plugs. He came in for a change of plugs and then the race was finished. But he could have won that first round easily.' Instead he was a dogged 13th, three laps in arrears.

Still, the speed was there. 'The Copersucar was very quick at Interlagos,' Emerson recalled. 'We thought it would be good everywhere. But our first surprise was Africa. We tested there and we couldn't make the bloody thing work.' During tyre tests at South Africa's Kyalami track, said Divila, 'we tried all these ideas from McLaren and the car went slower and slower.' 'We just couldn't believe it,' said Ramirez. 'Emerson changed everything – big things, the wheelbase, track – everything. After the first day of practice he was struggling to qualify.

'We had one more day of practice,' Ramirez continued. 'I remember telling Richard, "Now, we'll just have to be strong." I said to Emerson, "You've had your go and it didn't work. Let's put the car back the way it was at Interlagos and have another go at it." "Oh," he said, "you're wasting your time!" So we put the car back the way it was. And he was much faster the next day.' Problems with fried spark boxes – one borrowed from Team Surtees got him going – kept him from a good grid position. Emerson ran ninth in the race until his engine gave out eight laps from the finish. This, Divila admitted, was owing to his oil-tank design that 'wasn't perfect'.

It wasn't easy for the team to be strong with Emerson. 'Except for Jo,' said Divila, 'the rest of us were very young. You have to have respect for somebody who has been there' 'Richard wasn't strong enough to say, "No, I'm the engineer here, I call the shots,"' said Ramirez. 'It was Emerson's team, he was the boss. He was a great fiddler, but most drivers are. I suppose when you get to be World Champion you can allow yourself that. Even more so if you own the team, of course.'

Having stepped down as a driver, Wilson was still deeply committed to the team he'd launched, Ramirez added: 'Wilson's main role was getting the money and the sponsorship, but of course at race meetings he was very much involved. He wanted to make some technical decisions as well. But to give Wilson his due, he listened to Richard more.' The problems at Kyalami at the start of '76 saw the brothers at loggerheads: 'Wilson and Emerson had a blazing row at the pool,' Divila recalled. This was not unusual, added the engineer. 'The brothers would have a real set-to. It was quite fun to watch.'

'It was reasonable at Long Beach,' said Emerson of the FD04. There he and Stuck collided on lap two but Fittipaldi then battled his way through the field to finish sixth, winning his young team's first championship point. Spain at the beginning of May saw start-line excitement when a brake-fluid leak was spotted on Emerson's car. He was allowed to swap with Hoffman's non-qualifying car without losing his grid position, only to retire after three laps with gear-selection maladies.

The race at Jarama had seen a setback for the team from its tyre supplier, Goodyear. Lawsuits against the Akron giant had resulted from Mark Donohue's fatal crash at Austria the previous August, following a burst tyre. 'Goodyear went conservative,' said engineer Divila.

'At Spain they had a new six-ply tyre in place of the previous two-ply. McLaren and Ferrari had tested on them, but they didn't work on cars with less-loaded front wheels. They just didn't suit our cars, which understeered so much that you couldn't turn.'

From his mate Carlos Pace, Emerson learned that the Brabhams were running ultra-stiff springs. Brushing aside Divila's protestations that this only worked with their pull-rod-and-rocker suspension, the driver insisted on stiffer coils for his conventionally sprung racer for the next race at Zolder in Belgium. The result, said Divila, was that 'he was running too much on the edges of the tyres.' Emerson failed by a tenth of a second to make the 26-car field. A non-qualification for the double World Champion was a low point for the little squad.

The next race at Monaco was only a week away. Richard Divila hurried back to their British base after the qualification failure to make up some new bits and pieces, which they tested during the week in a session at Paul Ricard. 'We had a little bit of improvement,' said Ramirez. 'We went to Monaco, where we were very pleased with it.' The record shows that Fittipaldi easily qualified and collected another championship point with a fifth-place finish. 'I was taking more risks driving at the back than I did when I was out in front with the McLaren,' the driver recalled. 'To qualify seventh and finish sixth at Monaco I drove what I think was one of the finest races I ever drove in my life – and nobody knew it but me!'

This wasn't quite the case. In fact during qualifying his team had a close look at Emerson's efforts. Just minutes before the end of final practice, said team manager Ramirez, 'we were sort of struggling, about 17th or 18th on the 20-car grid, and he was very, very short of fuel. I was thinking, "God, will he have time and fuel for another lap or not? Shall I let him do it or shall I bring him in? Whatever I do he'll be upset."' Jo decided to leave him out, whereupon he was confronted by an irate Emerson sputtering into their pit. 'He opened his visor and he was furious. He shouted, "You cost me a good lap!"' A quick splash of petrol went in.

'He was so mad,' said Jo, 'that he took off sideways. Wilson was shouting, "Oh, God, he's going to kill himself," and I said, "No, forget it. Someone of his experience will probably do a good lap." And his first flying lap was a second and a half faster than he'd done the whole weekend.' For Ramirez this was a bittersweet result. 'I was devastated. I was really upset. We'd been working flat out. He was happy and smiling and I said, "Emerson, what are we doing? All we did was upset you and put in a gallon of fuel and you went more than a second faster! It doesn't matter how much effort, how much money you put in. If you don't put in the same effort on the track we're wasting our time – we all are."

'He was good,' Jo said of his response. 'He realised that he just hadn't been putting the effort in.' The problem, said Divila, was Emerson's tremendous natural speed: 'He always drove at 92 or 95 per cent. He had this huge safety margin, because he was *so fast*.' He had to be motivated – as he was for both practice and the race at Monaco – to delve into some or all of that margin. Ramirez had shown that he was willing to criticise his star driver, and indeed went even farther after Monaco by suggesting that they test with another driver to get a second opinion on the car. 'Jo almost got killed!' laughed Richard.

Jo almost killed his star driver after the British Grand Prix at Silverstone. The result was another sixth place and another point for the team, but Ramirez was angry about an incident during the race when Emerson was lapped by James Hunt's McLaren M23. 'Emerson was lapping two seconds slower,' Jo recalled, 'and when Hunt passed him he went right behind him and he started lapping a second faster and he stayed behind him for a couple of laps or so. Afterward I said, "Look at your times. Do you think you're a Sunday afternoon driver or what?" He was up and down during the whole year.'

'At Austria we found we had no top speed,' Emerson related of the mid-August race at the fast Österreichring. 'After that we tested our engine with our complete oil system on the McLaren dynamometer and found we were losing 20 horsepower because our system was holding too much oil in the crankcase. Then for Monza we installed new lighter magnesium front uprights and we had no front-wheel grip at all. There were no tyre temperatures! It was terrible.' He soldiered to a 15th-place finish two laps behind. No joy came in the final races of 1976, ending when Emerson joined Pace and

Lauda in withdrawing from the early laps of the rainy and misty Japanese Grand Prix.

For 1977 Emerson and Wilson turned to old friend Dave Baldwin, erstwhile designer for Lotus Components, to pen a new Fittipaldi. Baldwin, whom Emerson called 'a perfectionist,' had designed the 1976 Ensign for Mo Nunn's team. His similar F5 wasn't ready until mid-season, so Emerson started the year with the old FD04 – and in storming fashion. He was fourth in Argentina and fourth again in Brazil, a lap behind and helped by retirements. Ingo Hoffman even finished at Interlagos, a doughty seventh. In South Africa Emerson was tenth, the last finisher not to be lapped by the Ferrari of winner Lauda.

Improved form was confirmed at Long Beach in April with seventh place on the grid for Fittipaldi and fifth at the finish. The points were mounting up. But this proved a deceptive start to a year that saw points won in only one other race, the Dutch Grand Prix, where Emerson was fourth in his new F5 after strongly challenging Scheckter's Wolf for third. Many grid places were well back; Hockenheim and Monza saw failures to qualify and his entry for Fuji was withdrawn. Retirements were all too common. Nevertheless his strong early races placed Emerson 12th among the 20 points-scoring drivers and his team ninth among constructors.

'In 1978 I had a good year,' Emerson told Gordon Kirby, 'including a second in the Brazilian Grand Prix. The car was fast that year and I was enjoying driving.' His F5A's speed was helped by the arrival of designer Ralph Bellamy in the team and full-skirted ground effects on the Lotus model. Fittipaldi's second place at Jacarepagua near Rio behind Carlos Reutemann's Ferrari was an epic achievement, taken in searing heat in his spare car after his designated racer wouldn't start. It was as good as a win for his enthusiastic home crowd, which erupted when he passed pole-sitter Peterson's Lotus into third on the 12th lap. They went berserk when he stole second from Mario Andretti's faltering Lotus with only a handful of laps to go. Emerson had to stop half-way around his cooling-off lap to avoid his fans swarming onto the track, an updated version of the one on which the Fittipaldi brothers had raced their exotic homebuilt creations in the 1960s.

In '78 for the first time the Fittipaldi team entered one of the non-championship British Formula 1 races, the ones that Emerson had always felt were important precursors to the season. Silverstone in mid-March was so wet that some racers left the track during the parade lap. Emerson persevered in his F5A to finish second, after 117 miles only two seconds behind Keke Rosberg's Theodore.

From the summer, when Fittipaldi was sixth in Sweden, his season picked up pace. At Silverstone he was up to seventh before mid-race, only to have an engine let go. Now qualifying higher than mid-grid, Emerson was fourth at Hockenheim and again in Austria two weeks later, where the race was run in two parts after being stopped in torrential rain. At Zandvoort the Brazilian was fifth and at Watkins Glen he was fifth again, with an eighth at Monza in between. This was the terrible Italian Grand Prix that saw the death of Emerson's erstwhile team-mate Ronnie Peterson. In Canada Emerson qualified sixth fastest, only to be taken out in the first turn by a banzai-charging Hans Stuck.

Nineteen seventy-eight's results were a welcome whiff of promise for the Copersucar effort. Emerson was equal ninth in points with Gilles Villeneuve and the marque bearing his name was seventh among constructors, in fact two points ahead of his former employer McLaren. This was just good enough to encourage them to carry on with a new car, the F6, but it proved a disappointment, in spite of Emerson's efforts to develop it by racing it. The team's only points finish in 1979 was a sixth place in the season's first race in Argentina.

At the end of '79 the Fittipaldis took over the assets of another struggling Formula 1 team, that of the wealthy Canadian Walter Wolf. They acquired its Reading base, leading engineer Harvey Postlethwaite, team manager Peter Warr and a charging young Finnish driver, Keke Rosberg. The results in 1980 for new sponsor Skol lager were not too bad – equal seventh in constructors' points with McLaren and Arrows, comprising six points contributed by Rosberg and five by Emerson. The boss scored his with a sixth at Monaco – where Beatle George Harrison was in his pit – and a satisfying third place at Long Beach, where he shared the podium with a fellow Brazilian, Nelson Piquet.

Nineteen-eighty was Fittipaldi's last in Formula 1 and by no means his happiest. 'In 1979 and '80 the cars were a disaster,' he said, 'and I did not enjoy myself at all. Those two years were my last in Formula 1 and I was going to the races only because it was an obligation. I was too involved in the problems of trying to make the team work, and I neglected my marriage and my personal life. For me, it was a very, very bad time in my life. But when you have a bad experience you learn some lessons and, in this case, I learned many lessons. I learned that it's a big mistake to try and go racing if you don't have the money to do it properly.'

Fittipaldi decided to step out of the car and accept the role of team principal for the 1981 season, fielding both Rosberg and promising Brazilian Chico Serra. The year was a dead loss. In '82 the team entered a solitary car for Serra, who scored only a single point with sixth in the accident-plagued Belgian Grand Prix. Richard Divila rejoined Fittipaldi for that final season. 'During the last three years we were caught up in the problems of Brazil,' he recalled. The nation's notoriously fragile economics were again in turmoil, with 200-per cent inflation the norm. 'Any sponsorship we received was taxed by 30 per cent before it left Brazil. Everything that the Fittipaldis had earned before went back into the team. It became more of a chore than a pleasure.' Instead of managing the team, said driver Rosberg, Peter Warr 'was running a creditors' office from dawn to dusk. It took miracles to keep the ship afloat and it should have sunk long before it did.'

Why had the brothers persevered against such heavy odds? 'The pressure that was on the Fittipaldis in Brazil was immense,' said Divila. 'Everywhere you went somebody was commenting on them. It was in all the papers, all the news. It was worse than Ferrari in Italy. That influenced them. While what you need is stability and continuity, they were constantly making changes to try to get results. In the team, as well, we didn't stand back enough to see the whole picture.'

The onset of the ground-effects era and its technical repercussions wrong-footed the young team as well. 'I underestimated what it would take to build our own team,' Emerson admitted to Gordon Kirby, 'particularly with the constant technology in Formula 1 escalating so rapidly. I never thought it would be as difficult as it was. We were just unable to generate the financial and technical support we expected from Brazil. It was very disappointing.'

To boot, Fittipaldi hated the new ground-effect cars. 'He would come back to the hotel at night and we would talk a lot about the cars,' said his brother Wilson. 'He would say he no longer enjoyed the driving. Skill had gone out of it and his life depended on a four-foot piece of plastic staying on the road. The cars had lost their feel and he had lost his motivation to race.'

Outsiders judged that by the 1980 season, at the age of 33, Emerson Fittipaldi was washed up as a driver. They were wrong. His skills were still intact, but his desire was crushed by the cares of team ownership and his failure to meet the impossible demands of his countrymen. He was not forgotten by the leading teams; one extended him a feeler in 1982. That he did not respond to it was a sign of how demotivated he had become.

'He threw away one or two more World Championships,' said his friend and colleague Richard Divila. 'He didn't do what he could have done.' In Grand Prix racing this was certainly true. But Emerson was fated to rediscover his motivation and revive his astonishing skills in another sphere altogether.

Inevitably Emerson and Wilson Jnr., car fanatics from childhood, one day build a Formula 1 car of their own. Emerson later admits that setting up the company and the team was far more difficult than he had envisioned.

The first Copersucar-backed Fittipaldi Formula 1 car is built in the brothers' facility at Interlagos (above), including its aluminium monocoque (opposite top). Ready at the end of 1974, the sleek silver car is tested by Wilson Jnr. on the Interlagos track (below and opposite bottom). It is the beginning of a long road for the brothers.

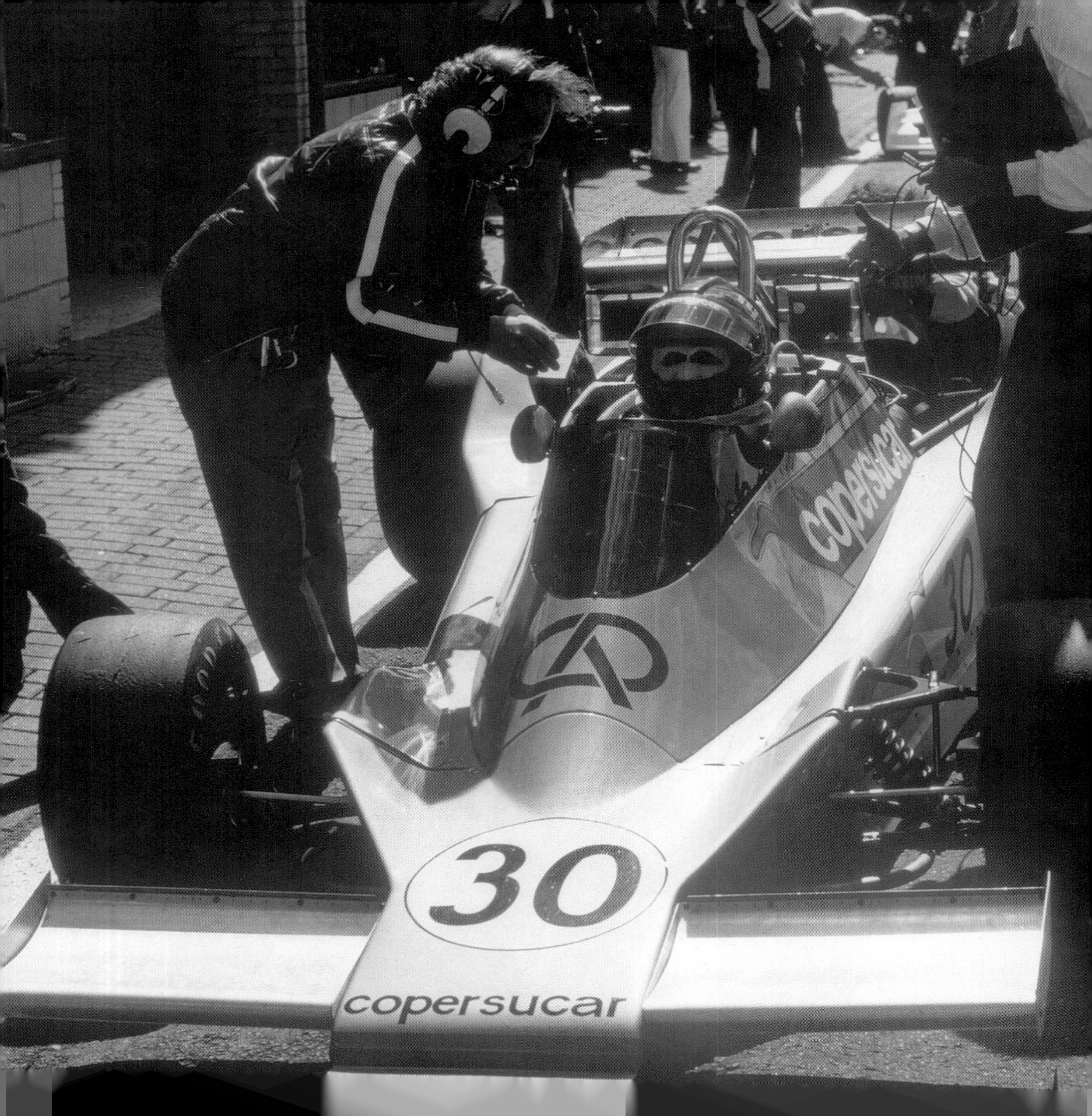

copersucar
30
30
copersucar

For 1976 Richard Divila designs a 'standard kit car' for Fittipaldi, the FD04, which encourages Emerson to join the team. He is competing with it at Zandvoort (opposite), Long Beach (above) and Monaco (below). In the latter two races he comes sixth, scoring points in both for his family enterprise.

Updated for 1977, the FD04 is still a useful racing car that takes Emerson to fifth place at Long Beach (opposite top). That year he finishes fourth three times. Monaco (above, opposite bottom and overleaf) sees retirement with engine problems.

With the close-knit Fittipaldis, racing is always a family affair. Father Wilson looks on while Emerson tugs off his gloves at Sweden in 1976, while Maria Helena contemplates the team's challenges at Monaco. At the Monegasque track in 1976 (opposite) Wilson and Emerson check the latest bulletins with team manager Jo Ramirez.

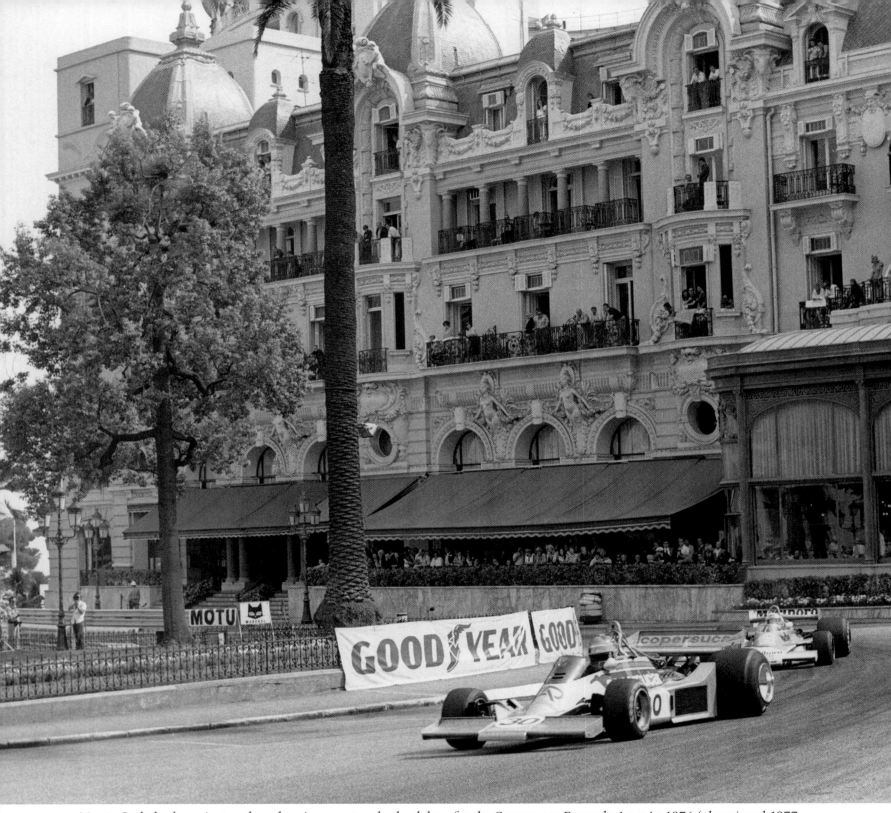

Monte Carlo both ancient and modern is a spectacular backdrop for the Copersucar Formula 1 car in 1976 (above) and 1977 (opposite). In 1976 Emerson is under attack from the McLaren of former team-mate Mass, who relegates the Brazilian to sixth (overleaf top). Seen approaching the tunnel in his F5A (overleaf bottom), his Copersucar's engine lets him down in 1979.

In his first season with the Fittipaldi-Copersucar team, 1976, Emerson waits patiently in the pits and discusses the state of play with a former Team Lotus colleague. Hopes and expectations are still high.

At a damp Zandvoort in 1976 Fittipaldi stretches his legs. He is less happy walking away from the Belgian Grand Prix in 1980. He is a classified finisher in only six races that season, his last in Formula 1.

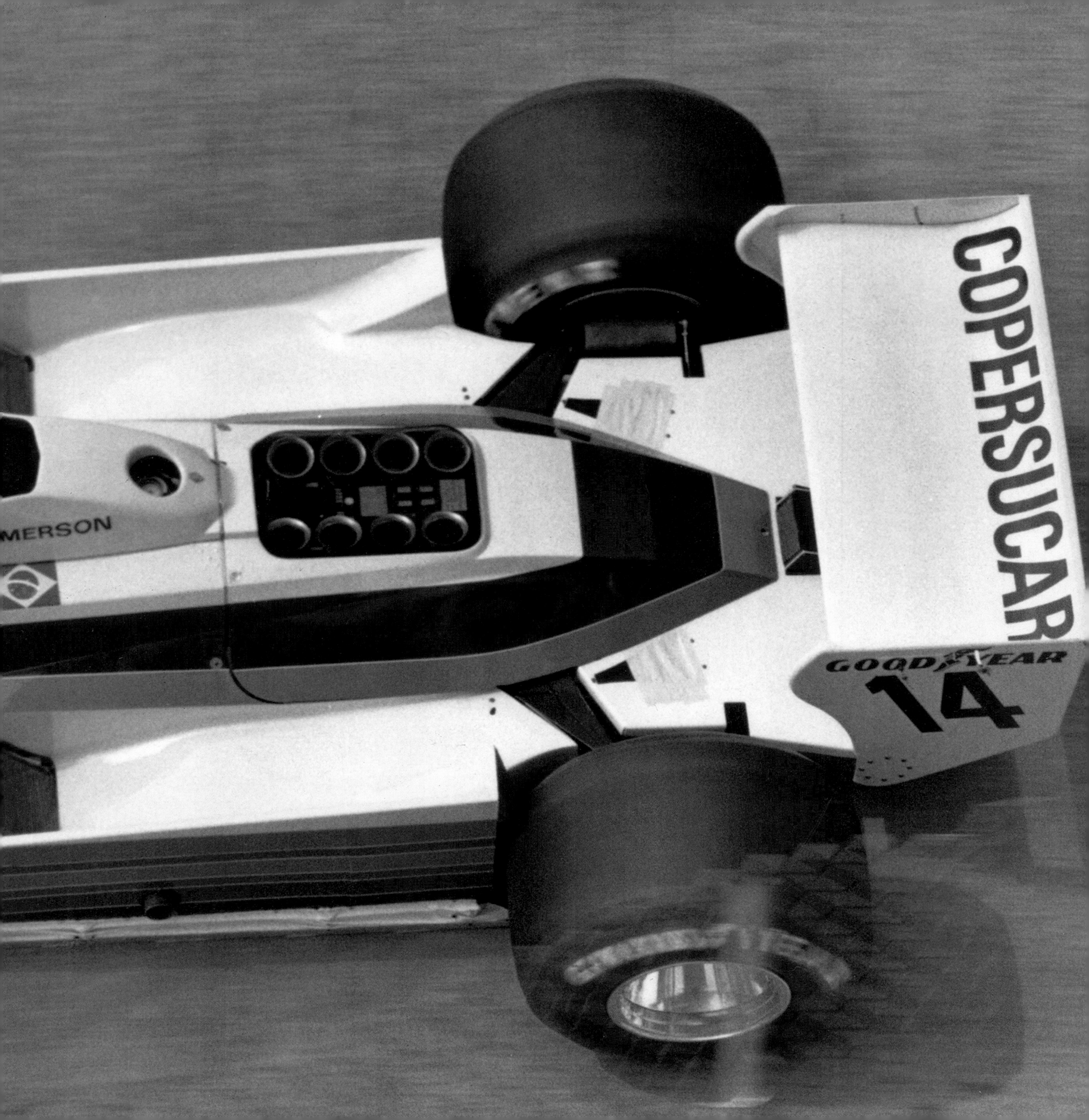
COPERSUCAR
MERSON
GOODYEAR
14

Frequent designer and design changes blunt the plucky Fittipaldi team's attack. In 1978 the F5A (above) is useful, placing second in Brazil and in the points five more times. The spectacular-looking 1979 F6 (preceding pages) proves a dead end and is succeeded by the ground-effects F7 (below), which takes Emerson to his last Grand Prix podium at Long Beach in 1980.

Publicly Emerson keeps his spirits high in the Copersucar years, but privately financial problems take their toll of his fabled enthusiasm. After 1980, in which his final points-scoring finish is a sixth at Monaco (overleaf), he deserts the cockpit and manages his declining team for two more dispiriting seasons.

CHAPTER 7

CARTing Champion

'In 1983 I started racing Super Karts with some friends in Brazil and that got me excited again about driving racing cars.' As simply as that Emerson Fittipaldi described the spark that reignited his enthusiasm for racing.

Naturally enough his thoughts turned to Formula 1. In January 1983 the Grand Prix teams came to Rio for a week of warm-weather testing of cars and tyres. Fittipaldi was there, looking them over. Skirts had been banned, he was happy to see. Drivers seemed more in control, not just passengers in cars sucked to the ground. Some were even opposite-locking to catch slides. This, thought Emerson, was more like it.

Super Karts were his next step. Twenty years after he'd first made his name in karting, Emerson settled back into one of these low-slung machines. He relished the speed, the cornering, the camaraderie with like-minded friends. 'I enjoyed it,' he said, 'and I found I was still very com-

Emerson Fittipaldi rides back into the pages of racing history in 1984 aboard a year-old March 83C Cosworth bankrolled by a consortium of Florida enthusiasts. In his first CART race it takes him to fifth at Long Beach (bottom). He is twelfth in his first-ever race on an oval at Phoenix (top). The 'Mouse' is back.

petitive against the young guys who were very good. I got excited again!' In '83 he travelled to Europe to talk to some Formula 1 teams, to see what was afoot.

Fittipaldi's desire to be at the wheel of a proper racing car again was so intense that he settled for a first outing at a level of Formula 1 racing that was so low as to be virtually subterranean. During the week of 16 January 1984 all the teams repaired to the circuit at Rio de Janeiro for a marathon session of car and tyre testing in 120°F heat. On deck was Emerson Fittipaldi, driving a Hart-engined Spirit, a car that looked as lashed-up as it was.

The Spirit came to Rio thanks to the backing of wannabe-Formula-1-racer Fulvio Ballabio, who was visibly at sea in this demanding milieu. In brief drives between those in which Ballabio damaged the car, Fittipaldi showed all his legendary speed and style. 'Now that I have driven again,' he said, 'I know I can race competitively. I am still getting used to the braking points and cornering speeds, but I already feel very comfortable in the car and every lap I feel better.'

The Spirit was manifestly not the vehicle that Fittipaldi needed in order 'to show people,' as his brother said, 'that he really wants to go racing again.' That vehicle was waiting for Emerson in Florida. It was a 1983 March-Chevrolet 83G, an IMSA GTP coupé owned by the brothers Al and Art Leon and rented to Ralph Sanchez, promoter of the Miami Grand Prix held over a brutal 1.9-mile 14-turn track on the harbour side of that Florida city.

For the second running of his three-hour race on 26 February 1984 the well-liked Sanchez wanted a special attraction, and he found it in Emerson Fittipaldi. In what was described by Steve Nickless as the Brazilian's 'brilliant comeback to big league motor racing,' Emerson put the March on the pole with a lap that was 'breathtaking, his vicious wheel-spinning slides off line caught as if by magic as Fittipaldi charged through traffic.' In the race he and co-driver Tony Garcia were challengers for the lead when a gearbox shaft broke less than an hour from the finish. The un-retired driver had made his mark, as *On Track* reported: 'Proving his years in retirement cost him none of his skills, Emerson Fittipaldi put on a show to remember.'

It was a show that won him the backing he needed for a racing comeback. The venue was neither Formula 1 nor IMSA. Instead it was America's CART Indycar championship, a series battled over road circuits and ovals large and small, including the famed Speedway at Indianapolis. Florida enthusiasts led by IMSA driver Jose 'Pepe' Romero banded together to create WIT Racing Promotions, which bought a year-old March-Cosworth for Emerson to drive – if he liked it. He met the March 83C on Tuesday, 13 March at California's Willow Springs road circuit. Although brake problems and a misfire kept him from posting a competitive time, Fittipaldi accepted the car. He decided to plunk for CART.

Emerson announced his decision the following day at a luncheon of California's Orange County sports journalists. 'I am at a good age to start again,' the 37-year-old told the writers. 'These last three years have been like recharging the battery. I hated those last years in Formula 1. Now I am ready to try to go racing again for the enjoyment. If success and money follow, it will be fantastic, but I want to enjoy the sport again. I miss it, you know – the sensations of driving fast cars and the competition.'

The luncheon was timed to whet appetites for the first Indycar race of the season on the Long Beach street circuit in California on the first of April. Even among the colourful CART campaigners, who were competing at Long Beach for the first time, Emerson stood out with his fuchsia March and his helmet, which he had redesigned with a striking orange motif radiating from its brow. His American fans welcomed him with cheers surpassed only by those awarded to hero Mario Andretti.

Andretti was the Long Beach winner but Fittipaldi made his presence known with his year-old March. Lining up 12th of 28 starters, he charged to the front and was bidding fair for a finish in second or third when he ran out of methanol and coasted in to make an extra stop. A problem with second gear – used five times around the circuit – was another handicap, but he finished fifth, two laps behind Mario.

Two weeks later his short-oval-track baptism at Phoenix was less heartening. His confidence in the inexperienced WIT team, already shaken by the Long Beach snafus and problems over his Indy entry, was further shaken by his car's failure to arrive in Arizona for the first practice. Though Fittipaldi's time on the one-mile oval wasn't quick enough to qualify, he was one of two entries admitted under the race promoter's option. Emerson finished 12th, seven laps off the winner's pace, albeit first rookie and first year-old-March driver. 'That was fantastic!' the Brazilian enthused about his Phoenix début. 'I have never experienced so much wheel-to-wheel racing in my life! But this is what gives me the motivation to come back. There is so much to learn, so many new things.'

Fittipaldi had a new March 84C in May for the Indy 500, where WIT's poor preparation let him down. Afterwards he fell out with WIT, which 'has not been conspicuously well organised, and the Brazilian's frustration has become more and more obvious.' This was not the atmosphere that the racing returnee hoped for. He suspended his comeback until he made a connection with Gary Bettenhausen's team, H&R Racing, to drive road courses. In July Emerson drove for H&R at the Meadowlands in New Jersey, placing seventh two laps back after a botched pit stop, and at Cleveland where he qualified a strong seventh but retired with an overheated Cosworth V8 after running as high as fourth.

It is a sad fact of motor racing that opportunities arise when another racer is killed or hurt. In 1970 Fittipaldi stepped into the sizeable shoes of the deceased Jochen Rindt at Lotus, and in 1984 he was available when Chip Ganassi, a star driver for oilman Pat Patrick's team, was severely injured in a high-speed crash on Michigan's two-mile banked oval. In the last week of July Emerson test-drove one of Patrick's Marches on Elkhart Lake's road course and set a time that matched the previous year's pole. In August he tested at the sinuous Mid-Ohio road course, where he made his début for the Patrick team on September 2nd. This was more like it. He qualified sixth and finished fourth two laps off the pace, hampered by a leg cramped by an ill-fitting cockpit.

On 24 August Pat Patrick had announced that Fittipaldi would join his team for the full 1985 season, racing alongside veteran Gordon Johncock. A taste of the challenges he would face was served up at Quebec's Sanair, a tight 0.8-mile tri-oval, a week after Mid-Ohio. Emerson qualified so poorly that he was only admitted as a promoter's choice and crashed out of the race after 155 of the 225 laps, evidently the victim of a punctured tyre, triggering a shunt by his team-mate behind him. In the next race on Michigan's oval Fittipaldi made haste slowly, both qualifying and finishing 12th.

Emerson took a break from several races before competing in the season finale on a 1.1-mile track in the parking lot of Ceasars Palace in Las Vegas. He qualified an excellent sixth and was a factor on the race until he was squeezed into a wall by his rival for rookie of the year, Roberto Guerrero. The latter took that honour, with Fittipaldi finishing second. With points from five races in his début season Emerson was 15th in the final CART PPG standings.

The 1985 season saw Emerson contesting all 15 rounds of the CART series for Pat Patrick's team in 85C Marches. It was a season, said *Autosport* with thinly disguised condescension, in which the Brazilian 'should get the chance to demonstrate whether or not he can make it as an Indycar driver' – as if his '84 races hadn't made that clear. He moved quickly to stake his claim with a second-place finish at Long Beach behind Mario Andretti. He was eighth on the Milwaukee oval after Indy, third at Portland and second again at the Meadowlands before falling to eighth on Cleveland's Lakefront Airport track.

On 28 July 1985 the CART circus decamped at Michigan International for its 500-mile race. As usual on this fast track, attrition was high from both crashes and engine failures. Fittipaldi was a survivor, however. 'I had fought through and taken the lead, then I pulled clear,' he recalled. 'It was one of those days when everything went right – tyres, pit stops, working the traffic. Then everything went wrong with the yellow right at the very end. The track went green with a lap to go, and there right behind me was Al Unser Snr. All round that lap I was flat. I had never taken that chance before, and here was Big Al right behind me! The oval expert! I thought for sure he'd pass me. But I finished in front with him still right on my gearbox.' His winning margin was a scant tenth of a second.

'A fantastic moment for me,' said the ecstatic victor. Fantastic indeed, for the Brazilian 'retread' had won his first CART race, his 16th since taking up this new sport. It wasn't quite so quick a start as he'd made in Formula 1, but then CART racing was ultra-competitive with eight different drivers scoring wins during the season. After finishing fifth in his next outing at Elkhart Lake, Emerson found himself tied for the championship lead with another former Team Lotus driver, Mario Andretti. Both fell out of the points race in the latter part of the season. With ten finishes in the top ten, Fittipaldi ended 1985 sixth in the CART ranking.

Emerson continued with the Patrick team for the next four seasons, through 1989. In 1986 Gordon Kirby considered that the Brazilian had 'fully established himself after three years of his comeback as a top-class, all-round Indycar driver.' He added that in '86 Emerson was 'tremendously unlucky through the middle of the season' with 'two or three "should haves" taken away by mechanical failure.' He seized his first qualifying poles on road courses at Toronto and Portland. Best of all he scored another win on that great road course in Wisconsin, Elkhart Lake, this time with a 0.3-second margin over Michael Andretti in a wet race. This plus four podium finishes placed Fittipaldi seventh in that year's championship.

For the 1987 season the Patrick team gambled by fitting the new Ilmor-built Chevrolet Indy engines, which were strong on power but suffered from debilitating torsional vibrations. Emerson lost an engine while leading at Portland and retired all too often elsewhere, leaving him only tenth in points for the season. His Chevys stayed together for brilliant back-to-back victories at Cleveland and Toronto, however.

In a season post-mortem, Emerson and Pat Patrick met with Ilmor's engineers to discuss their Chevy's chequered performance. 'You've got a fantastic engine there,' Fittipaldi told them, 'but it just has to finish races. If it doesn't, we will have to change engines.' They replied that they had a handle on the problem, and indeed they did. In 1988 this was of maximum benefit to the Penske CART team, which dominated that year's results. Switching during the season from a March chassis to a Lola, however, Emerson again scored successive victories on road courses, this time at Mid-Ohio and Elkhart Lake. He was third at Portland and on Milwaukee's oval, and second on the road course at Florida's Tamiami Park. His successes added up to seventh in the CART championship.

Fittipaldi's 1989 and '90 seasons were linked by a swap between Roger Penske and Pat Patrick at the behest of sponsor Marlboro. 'Marlboro wanted to come to Penske,' said the latter team's Teddy Mayer, 'and that deal was done almost two years in advance. They told Pat they were going to Penske and they made the deal to get Emerson into one of our cars.' The deal was that in exchange for relinquishing Marlboro sponsorship, the Patrick team would get brand-new current-season PC18 Penske racing cars for its 1989 campaign.

With quality equipment at his disposal, Emerson decided to get his own act together. Hitherto he hadn't been wholeheartedly committed to CART. He and Wilson were keeping their business balls in the air in Brazil while the younger brother was racing in America. 'Even after he got out of the race car he was working,' said his nutritionist Gary Smith. 'He was on his cell phone talking to Brazil and then he would get in his race car and go qualify it. He never took a break. And it was affecting him.' For 1989 he buckled down to concentrate on his fitness and dedicate himself to the full CART season with Patrick.

Emerson had what was called a 'dream season' in 1989. Including the Indianapolis 500-mile race – which he won – he started from pole four times, from the front row nine times and won five races. Of 2,057 available race laps he led 584. In addition to Indy his wins came at Detroit, Portland, Cleveland and Nazareth, bringing to a record $2,166,078 his winnings for the year. From the Detroit race in mid-June he was the championship leader, a position he never relinquished, adding a CART PPG title to his Indy win and two Formula 1 World Championships. 'In view of his mastery of oval track racing,' wrote Gordon Kirby, 'Fittipaldi is now clearly the most complete Brazilian racing driver the world has ever seen.'

This was the man, 'truly revitalised in both his personal and professional lives,' who was presented together with Danny Sullivan and Rick Mears at a press conference in New York on 24 October 1989 as a member of a Penske 'superteam' for 1990. At Penske he was reunited with Teddy Mayer, whose determination and commitment he had admired during his McLaren years in 1974–75. 'This was very enjoyable for me,' said Mayer. 'He was a good guy to work with, very clear as to what the car did when you'd made a change, very helpful in telling you what he needed, what would make the car go faster where he was not quick. A very good sound racing mind.'

Superteam or not, the Penske outfit struggled in 1990 and, with it, the career of its Brazilian driver wearing the number 1 that symbolised his status as reigning champion. He started from pole in the two fastest races at Indy and Michigan but could win neither. Two seconds and three thirds came his way but not until the season's penultimate race on Nazareth's one-mile oval could Fittipaldi score a win. In CART points he was fifth in 1990 and again in 1991, when by winning at Detroit he became the sixth different victor in the first six events, tying an Indycar record set in 1959.

Emerson opened his 1992 account for Penske with a bang, leading team-mate Rick Mears in the now-two-car team to a win at Surfer's Paradise in Australia. More victories came at Elkhart Lake, Mid-Ohio and Cleveland, where he started on pole and led 67 of the 85 laps. His successes would accrue to fourth in the 1992 points standings.

The win at Mid-Ohio came on 13 September, just twenty years since the weekend on which he'd won his first World Championship with Lotus. Near the end of the race at Mid-Ohio, the 45-year-old said, 'I had a gap on Paul Tracy and Al Unser Jnr. of about fifteen seconds, but it was difficult to concentrate because I was getting emotional thinking about what happened twenty years before. For the first time that weekend I called Roger Penske on my radio. I'd been too scared to say anything to the crew, but then I came on and told them. There was a lap to go but I took a chance! They all went mad and cheered! They screamed down the radio to congratulate me, which was a fantastic bonus.' At the flag he still had ten seconds in hand.

In October 1992, on the Saturday before the Sunday CART contest, Marlboro organised its annual Challenge race on the one-mile Nazareth oval. This was run as a 100-lap million-dollar dash including a mandatory stop for new tyres and fuel, with $300,000 to the winner. Eligible to race were the preceding year's race winners and pole-sitters. Emerson had done well in these Marlboro races previously, but in 1992 he won. 'The car was fantastic,' he said afterward. 'Early in the race I couldn't pass, but the car was working really well. I was just keeping the pressure on. Sometimes I would lose a little time in traffic, but I was always able to catch right up. We also had a very quick pit stop.'

Late in 1992 Fittipaldi tested the new PC22 he would race for the Penske outfit in 1993. In those tests he was joined by a fellow Brazilian, Ayrton Senna. This came about, Emerson said, after the two had dined together in Brazil: 'We exchanged some ideas, and I said to Ayrton, "Why don't you come over to the test in Phoenix? You can see the car and try it out." I called Roger Penske from Sao Paulo. He was a little concerned with the reaction from the press and everybody, but Roger was a great racing driver, a champion. He understood the position. Roger was very good on letting the whole situation happen, and very open for the future with Ayrton.'

Senna was between contracts at the time, so his test of a 1992 Penske-Chevy was provocative for the worlds of both Formula 1 and Indycars. He praised Fittipaldi's pioneering role: 'Emerson has been the man who has opened the doors in Formula 1 for most Brazilians,

including myself. When he was winning championships and races back in the 1970s, I was a go-kart driver who watched F1 races every Sunday on television. He motivated me to go out and eventually get to Formula 1.'

The test was on 20 December 1992 at Firebird Raceway, a sinuous road course grafted onto a drag strip. After a briefing from Emerson, Ayrton took to the track. 'He certainly knew how to drive a race car,' said the Penske team's Teddy Mayer. 'Ayrton was unbelievably quick right away. I mean *unbelievably* quick. And I really mean *right away*, instantly. I think it impressed Emerson!' 'Watching him drive was beautiful,' said Fittipaldi. 'He was smooth out of the corners. He put on a great show.'

Senna turned 25 laps at Firebird and stayed for two days to watch Fittipaldi shaking down his next season's PC22 at the Phoenix one-mile oval. He and his colleagues were motivated to be well prepared, because 1993 was the season that saw current Formula 1 champion Nigel Mansell invading CART. In the first race in Australia Mansell laid down his challenge by beating the 1972–74 World Champion by a scant five seconds.

With team-mate Paul Tracy, Fittipaldi kept Mansell honest in 1993. Another Indy win went into the Brazilian's golden book, while a win at Portland and seconds at Cleveland and Toronto (where he was on pole) put him in the lead for CART's championship. In August he was third in a 211-mile race at the 1-mile New Hampshire International Speedway that winner Mansell called 'one of the three best of my career.'

'The race at New Hampshire was probably the best motor race I've ever seen,' said Penske's Teddy Mayer. 'A helluva motor race between Mansell and Paul Tracy, running very, very close the whole time. Emerson wasn't far out of it; just at the very end he dropped back a tiny little bit. It was an incredible motor race.' This was seconded by Gordon Kirby, who wrote that 'the race in New Hampshire was as fine an advertisement for Indycar racing as you could ask for, with Mansell, Paul Tracy and Fittipaldi putting fearfully dramatic moves on each other in a magnificent fight to the finish … the final laps provided a great three-way conflict.'

In the season finale at Laguna Seca Fittipaldi was on pole and finished second, to be ranked second in the championship behind the carpetbagging Mansell. It was a pretty fair country season for a driver who completed 2,024 of the 2,112 available laps, and enjoyed nine podium finishes and totted up record earnings for a single season of $2,575,554.

The CART vice-championship was Emerson's lot in 1994 as well, achieved with one win at Phoenix, four seconds and five thirds. Two pole positions testified to his speed and determination. His Phoenix victory meant that 'Emmo', as his new fans hailed him, had won Indycar races in ten seasons in a row – a remarkable record. In '94 he was a top-ten finisher ten times.

Fittipaldi stretched that record to eleven years in a row with a win at Nazareth in April, 1995. By now he was 48 years old in a season in which a Canadian newcomer half his age, Jacques Villeneuve, won the CART title. Now using Ilmor-built Mercedes-Benz engines, Emerson was third at Phoenix but ended up with his worst career points standing in eleventh. 'It had been a very tough year for us,' he said, 'my most difficult year in Indycar racing.' But he was not ready to give up: 'It's very enjoyable when the car's going well. I still love it.'

For 1996 Fittipaldi was in a Penske-affiliated team, as Teddy Mayer explained: 'We had a plethora of people and Emerson was a little bit on the wane, I would say, but wanted to keep going. Carl Hogan wanted to run a team and Roger helped out with quite a bit of support. We provided pretty much the whole facility and Carl paid for some of it.' In the season's fifth race at Nazareth Emerson was on the CART radar screen for the first time that year with a fourth-place finish, which he matched at Milwaukee in June.

On 28 July Fittipaldi qualified well for the 500-mile race at ultra-fast Michigan International, scene of his first CART victory ten years earlier. 'The cars came up to speed and entered Turn One,' said an eyewitness. 'Then there was a fireball which slid through Two into the back straightaway. As the Indy safety crew rushed to the scene there was debris everywhere and what was left of a red car sat on the track. Half the field was running red cars and it took a few minutes to realise it was Emmo. As the yellow dragged on lap after lap, the safety crew continued to work to get Emmo out of the car. He was alive and conscious and yelling to his crew on the radio to get him out and complaining of back pain.'

'I had the impression that he was trying to climb out of the car,' said Teddy Mayer, 'and if he'd done that successfully he might have been in more trouble than he was in, which was plenty. He hit the wall very hard and had spinal injuries. They took him to the infield hospital first, then helicoptered him off to Foote Hospital in Jackson.' There his condition was stabilised before he was airlifted to Miami's Jackson Memorial Hospital, where he underwent an eight-hour operation. He had hit the wall at more than 200 mph with the force of 100 times gravity, an impact thought too severe to survive.

At the age of 49, Emerson Fittipaldi's racing days were over. He had won 22 Indycar races, 14th on the all-time list and tied with the great Tony Bettenhausen. He ranked fourth in total CART winnings with $14,293,625. Best of all, he was still alive. He had relished his new career in America: 'I loved it for the sport. It was like it was back in Formula 1 in the '70s. It was relaxed. There weren't the politics like there are in Formula 1. People were here because they love the sport. They settle the challenge on the track. They don't need to do it out of the car.'

In his first race for Texas oilman Pat Patrick at Long Beach in April 1985, Fittipaldi finishes a sensational second in his March 85C. Patrick and Fittipaldi remain teamed for half a decade.

Although Emerson enjoys Laguna Seca's hilly and twisty road circuit, it is not always lucky for him. In Patrick's March-Cosworths he is seventh in 1986 (above) and retires (opposite) in 1987. Now with Marlboro sponsorship, he is stopped at Long Beach in April 1986 (overleaf) by turbocharger waste-gate problems.

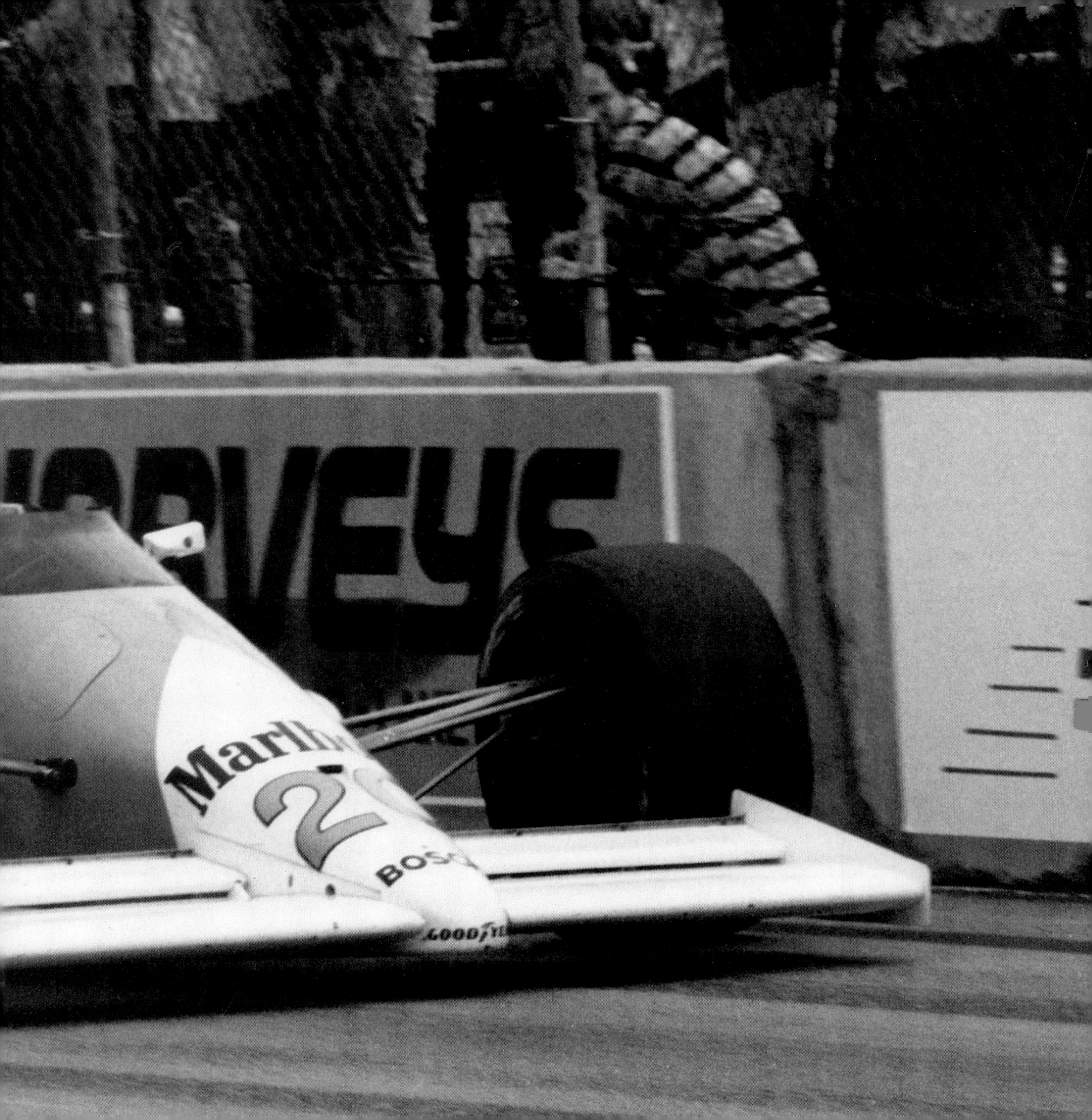

Tackling his 1989 CART season with renewed fitness, focus and dedication, Emerson Fittipaldi reaps the rewards. Driving Penske-Chevrolets for Patrick in a deal with Roger Penske's team, Fittipaldi wins five races – including the Indianapolis 500 – on his way to the 1989 CART championship.

Taking his Marlboro sponsorship with him to Team Penske in 1990, Emerson is fifth in the CART standings that year and in 1991. Driving the Chevrolet-powered Penske PC20, he is seen competing at Laguna Seca (preceding pages and above) and at Long Beach (opposite). In 1992, snapped by Bob Tronolone at Phoenix (overleaf), Fittipaldi scores four wins and is fourth in CART points.

Pictured on the street circuit at Long Beach in 1992 (overleaf) and 1993 (opposite), Fittipaldi wins three races including Indy in 1993 finishing second in CART points. In his Penske PC22-Chevrolet he is coping easily with traffic on the Phoenix oval in 1993 (above).

In 1990 reigning CART champion Emerson races to second at Long Beach in his Penske PC19. By 1995 the brilliant Fittipaldi has won CART races in eleven straight seasons.

CHAPTER 8

Iron-Fisted Pit Male

Making anagrams from the unusual name of Emerson Fittipaldi gives the apt title of this chapter. Other renditions include 'Pedal? Minister of it,' 'A fine pits old-timer' and 'Top life in a red mist' – all depictions that admirably suit this racing driver at various stages of his career. In fact 'red mist' may suit him the least, for there can be few World Champions whose tigerish attack on the circuit contrasted more with their relaxed demeanour away from the races. Fittipaldi could be laid-back to the point of horizontal.

His timekeeping was one manifestation. 'There's on time, late Brazilian time and Emerson time,' said Teddy Mayer in this book's Foreword. Brazilian time is movable but Emerson time is *late*. That was very consistent, right throughout his career. But the team managed to get around it. He was quite reliable about fulfilling his duties to sponsors and the like – late but reliable. Eoin Young gave another example: 'Breakfast for

In the first round of contests in the inaugural International Race of Champions series of 1973–74 at Riverside, Fittipaldi is well to the fore in Porsche number 12. In both his racing lives Fittipaldi is an active and respected IROC participant.

Emerson is a meal taken at an infinitely adjustable time prior to lunch. And if the two meals seem to be in danger of clashing, then lunch will be put back an hour or so.'

Eating and sleeping were two activities for which Fittipaldi allocated plenty of time. 'I like to sleep ten to eleven hours,' he told Elizabeth Hayward. 'Getting up at 10.30 in the morning is like waking at dawn. I really *like* sleep, and I think it is important to keep relaxed and for the body to recover all the strength that it loses in a day. And then I like to have a big breakfast every morning. I am the slowest eater in the world. The stomach works better if you eat slowly and don't rush. I'm sure my idea must be right, because I have always eaten a lot and I never get fat!'

Emerson's serenity carried over to his attitude on the track, as Hayward learned from Lotus mechanic Eddie Dennis: 'His calmness must help him enormously in his work. On the grid, where you see little bits of nervousness showing on other drivers – moving their hands, fiddling with the mirrors, feeling the switches – Emerson does nothing like that at all. He just sits there waiting for you to tell him when to start the engine. He doesn't start up when everyone else does. He doesn't necessarily follow suit; he just stays very calm indeed.'

'I don't think I'm a driver with a Latin temperament,' said the man himself. 'Not now, at least. I drove differently before going to England, but there I learned a lot about how to drive and how much risk to take.' Thrust into the limelight as he was with his first championship run in 1972, Fittipaldi struggled to cope with the concomitant pressures. 'There's so many things that you have to do,' he said at the time, that 'you should have a 36-hour day, not a 12-hour day. I have a lot of pressure now. On racing weekends it's difficult for a person to concentrate. But you have to. Because if you don't concentrate on the racing there's just no way that you can go quickly. Before the race I like to be on my own, but there's always someone under your feet talking to you. As soon as I get into the car I'm very calm, even if five minutes earlier I was irritated by all those people asking me questions.'

Here we had the very antithesis of the stereotype Latin racing driver, uncommon calm and composure being qualities that Emerson shared with that other great South American racer, Juan Fangio. They were certainly attractive to the first Mrs. Fittipaldi. 'He's very sympathetic and gentle' said Maria Helena. 'He's a romantic and kind man when he's away from the track.' Born to an English family living in Brazil, the gracious and charming Maria Helena was educated in both England and Switzerland. Her life changed when she met the Fittipaldis while staffing a check-in counter at the Sao Paulo airport.

'When I met Emerson in 1969,' she said, 'I knew nothing about motor racing. In my eyes he was a superman, very calm, friendly and natural. Emerson is a happy person by nature. He's also very positive. We married three months after we met' – on the last day of March 1970. 'When he took me to the first race I didn't know how skilled he was,' she added. 'I only realised how clever he was when he was asked to test a Lotus at Silverstone. If I had to describe my husband in a few words I would say he was tall, dark, with long hair and the nicest smile I've ever seen in my whole life.'

The fraternal Fittipaldi couples shared a villa in Sao Paulo's Morumbi district and a rented chalet in Switzerland during the racing season. At Morumbi a large room was devoted to the trophies of both Emerson and Wilson. Every two weeks the trophies were cleaned, a task which took two people two days. There and elsewhere in Sao Paulo the brothers kept their racing cars. By 1974 they had eight, including Tyrrell 002, an ex-Rob Walker Lotus 72, Formula 1 Marches from 1971 and '72 and the BT34 'lobster claw' model that Wilson drove for the Brabham works team. Various Indycars were subsequently added to the collection.

The young couple's hopes for an early addition to their family were dashed by the tragic car crash in France in 1971. In 1974, however, Emerson arrived at the Österreichring for the Austrian GP in high good humour, the reason for which was explained by a card which Maria Helena distributed. In telegraphic format it read as follows:

THE 1974 GRAND PRIX WHICH TOOK PLACE IN LAUSANNE-SUISSE AT THE HOSPITAL CANTONAL LAUSANNE ON 17 JULY WAS WON BY JULIANA FITTIPALDI WHO CROSSED THE FINISH LINE ALONE AT 8:33'17"

Juliana's details were specified as 'length: 46cm; weight: 2,990gm; fuel: Café do Brasil; accessories: standard equipment.' Next to arrive was a son, Jayson.

Aware as she was of his open and trusting demeanour, Maria Helena would caution Emerson not to take everyone at face value. 'He's very gentle with me,' she said. 'However I tell him not to be with others, as I think some people take advantage of him.' Their relationship suffered during the troubled Copersucar years, when by his own testimony Fittipaldi wasn't nurturing his marital relationship. By the end of that era his first marriage was over as well.

A colleague of Fittipaldi's remembered his *modus operandi* during those Grand Prix years. 'Emerson had two sorts of entourage,' he said. 'When he came to a race he would be accompanied by his wife and kids and manager and friends and father and mother – God knows who – all sorts of people. They were all very nice, but from time to time there were quite a few of them. That's what I would call the "entourage".

'But when he came testing,' the colleague continued, 'he would quite often bring a young lady who would hang around the back in the pit garage very quietly. She would disappear when Emerson disappeared and we knew nothing about it. She was definitely not always the same lady. It was all very discreet and done sensibly and quietly and not in anybody's face, but he did like his little bit of playing. He was definitely what we would call a player, not a spectator.'

Fitness was always a Fittipaldi fixation. His family had a house near the beach at Sao Paulo's getaway resort, Guarujà on the Atlantic coast. His routine there included a four-mile morning run on the beach, a long swim in the ocean and hours on the paddle-tennis court. During his break from racing in the early 1980s he kept in shape by working out in a Sao Paulo gym. There the newly single retired racer met a fellow keep-fit enthusiast, Teresa. They hit it off and were soon an item. When Emerson committed to a career in America they married and settled in Key Biscayne, an idyllic and exclusive island off the coast of Miami, Florida. Two daughters, Tatiana and Joana, and a son, Luca, were the fruits of this second marriage.

'They work hard and they play hard,' recalled Jo Ramirez of the Florida-based Fittipaldis. 'He enjoys life to the full. He did have a good sense of humour. They had a lovely house in Miami and I remember going to a party where everybody had to be in drag – you had to come dressed as a woman. He met most of my family at Indianapolis when it was my farewell party from McLaren. He recognised some of my brothers and sisters-in-law.'

Teresa Fittipaldi was an enthusiastic backer of her husband's revived career behind the wheel. In Brazil, especially in its north-eastern states, the voodoo religion is taken seriously, and Teresa was a practitioner. 'When Emerson would be leading a race, or hanging on for second or something,' said Teddy Mayer, 'she would stand in the pits and give them the evil eye or the double whammy – there's a witchcraft term for it – to whomever his competition was. We used to giggle quietly but hoped it worked!

'She was a lovely lady,' Mayer added. 'I liked Teresa. A very strong personality. She and Emerson had some ups and downs, because she was no carpet.' Teresa Fittipaldi expressed her independence with the design and sale of her own range of jewellery, which became popular among other racers' wives. After Fittipaldi hung up his helmet for good, the attractions of Key Biscayne paled for Teresa. 'When Emerson quit racing,' said Teddy Mayer, 'she wanted to go back to Brazil and *went*. And Emerson didn't go back for about another year.'

Eldest offspring Juliana has since presented Fittipaldi with two grandchildren. Juliana accompanied Emerson when he was invited to return to Indianapolis to be feted as a Legend of the Speedway in 2000. Uncharacteristically he awoke at 4.30 in the morning. Searching for something to do, he pulled on his running shoes and left the Speedway Motel to run some laps of the new 2.6-mile road course that would be used for the US Grand Prix for the first time that September.

'My daughter asked me, did I miss not driving?' he said in an Indy interview. 'Yes, but I recognise my age. I'd like to be younger, for sure, to be driving. Yes, I miss not driving, but I'm not frustrated. I'm very happy to be here. When I landed here, I started thinking how many days and months of my life I spent in Indianapolis. And I appreciate every minute I was here. Historically, since the beginning of the last century, so many people have been sweating, performing, driving to the edge to win here – different generations, different drivers and different nationalities. I was very proud to be a little part of Indianapolis.'

Tempting fate to do her worst, before the race at Michigan in 1996 that ended his career with a fiery crash, Emerson had told Roger Penske that he planned to retire at the end of that season. Fittipaldi had often spoken of retirement before. 'I think I'll retire at 30 years of age,' he said in 1972, when he was 25 and Europe-based during the season. 'I always look forward to going back to Sao Paulo to catch the sun and swim. Travelling is enjoyable, but it's tiring in the end. I definitely think I'll retire at 30.' By the time he turned 30, of course, he had a fresh challenge in his own Grand Prix car and team.

For a man with the heart of a racer, the pull of the sport was always greater than the attractions of retirement. This placed heavy demands on his fitness regime as he moved well into his 40s. 'I improved a lot in my physical training programme with Jim Landis,' he told Gordon Kirby in 1990. 'Different areas of the body where the driver requires effort, like the shoulder, the upper body, the arms. And I improved in the cardiovascular, trying to keep the stamina for the race. I work out every day back in Miami. I think it's more important, with more age, to keep up. I have to be in good condition, and to be in good condition you have to work hard. You have to dedicate yourself.' Emerson's fitness was given substantial credit for his survival of the Michigan crash in 1996.

'I consider myself lucky to be able to do this,' Fittipaldi said at the age of 43. 'I like to do it. I want to continue. I don't know for how many years, but as long as I'm competitive, I'll do it. I believe that in today's world you have so much risk outside of racing for anyone – my children, my wife, my parents, you and your family. Any time you leave home, you never know what can happen. My philosophy is you also have to have luck, and then luck will help you.' This philosophy helped him cope with his failure to qualify at Indy in 1995. He took it as a sign that he should not be in that year's race: 'I am not supposed to be in this race. I am not supposed to start in this race for whatever reason.' He returned instead to be a spectator – for the first time – at the Memorial Day event.

Twice Emerson took fate into his own hands by refusing to compete. The first occasion was at a Mallory Park Formula Ford meeting in October, 1969. 'I had trouble with the brakes and the steering,' Fittipaldi told Elizabeth Hayward. 'I didn't want to race the car in that condition. There are two things on a racing car for which I stop immediately, the steering and the brakes. If there is something wrong, if I know there's a failure of the brakes, then I come in at once. So I decided not to race. It was a difficult decision, when it was so important to catch up on points, but I never believed in taking risks. I said: "I'm not going to race a car when I'm not sure what will happen to it." And I did not race.'

The second such incident was the April 1975 Spanish Grand Prix on roads in Barcelona's Monjuich Park. When inspection showed the temporary Armco barriers to be anchored casually or not at all, Fittipaldi led the drivers in sitting out the Friday and Saturday morning practice sessions. Emerson judged the efforts at repair to be insufficient. 'He didn't like the general safety there at all and he was quite right,' said Teddy Mayer. 'They weren't

doing enough about it.' When practice finally started, wrote Peter Windsor, 'Fittipaldi did six very slow laps to ensure his McLaren wouldn't be impounded, climbed out of the car then announced that he wouldn't be driving again that weekend.'

'Nothing – money, contracts, racing – nothing is more important than safety,' said the reigning World Champion. 'My life was more important than money. I believe the track is not safe for racing and I hope the stand that I am making now will in some way help the safety situation.' The race went ahead without him, though he'd hoped his colleagues would have joined him in protest. 'I am very disappointed with my fellow drivers because we had been pushing hard for security and safety and I cannot understand why the drivers decided to go ahead and race. Everyone is a bit at fault – the drivers themselves as well as the organisers but most of all the CSI, because they had the last word and voted the race should go ahead.'

On lap 26 of 75 in Spain a heavy crash ensued when Rolf Stommelen's Lola-built Hill lost its rear wing, collected Carlos Pace and cannoned into the barriers, killing five people. 'This is what I feared would happen,' said Emerson. 'It is disgraceful. The track was just not safe enough. I am very, very, very upset. I still can't think why it should have been allowed to happen.

'To be a good racing driver,' Fittipaldi said, 'you have to be brave and you have to be afraid. You have to balance the brave and the afraid.' He suppressed the fear by using the best racing kit he could find. 'I have always tried to get the best equipment available for drivers,' he told Elizabeth Hayward. 'If there were new overalls or new helmets, to improve safety, I'd always be the first one in Brazil to have them. I think it is only sensible. I was one of the first people in Brazil to use fireproof overalls. Nobody in Brazil cared about seat belts or proper helmets or anything. They were not safety conscious then.'

Formula 1's followers are fascinated by how few accidents Emerson had during his long Grand Prix career, numbering 144 races – a career that began in an era when crashes and injuries were not that uncommon. For this driver even a spin was unusual. His safety record in 195 CART appearances was no less impressive. The answer lay in his uncommon ability, as Richard Divila remarked earlier: 'He had this huge safety margin, because he was *so fast*. He always drove at 92 or 95 per cent.' His brother Wilson agreed: 'My brother has a natural instinct. He gets into a single-seater car and immediately drives off at speed, great speed. I can probably drive as fast, but I need a lot more time to get used to the car. His is a natural gift, while I have to work hard to achieve the same things.'

In the cockpit, time seemed to move slowly for Fittipaldi. He seemed to be able to make maximum use of every fraction of a second in just the way he wanted. Although a quality shared with some other drivers, it seemed pronounced in his case. His was a remarkable ability to see what was happening at all times and – just as importantly – to be doing something about it.

Over and above his natural speed, Emerson evolved his style. In his early days, he said, 'I always liked to drive an oversteering car, to slide it, because I *enjoy* driving like that.' However, with the help of Colin Chapman he soon learned that this wasn't necessarily the fastest way. 'Sliding the car, it doesn't go quickly! Sometimes it's more controllable, but not so quick. Normally I use a very soft rear roll bar, to get as much grip as I can for the back of the car. And I drive a bit differently when the car is set up this way. When the other drivers drove my car, on my settings, they said, "The car is understeering very badly! You have to change the car!"' By matching his style to the needs of the car, Fittipaldi was faster.

He honed these skills in private testing. 'It takes a long time, many hours of testing, to get a Formula 1 car to work right,' he said, 'to work on the limit. That's why it is important to come before the official practice. Because in the official practice everybody is looking at the stop-watch, waiting, expecting the driver to go quicker! The team manager isn't thinking of what he can do to improve the car. He just thinks, "Oh, somebody else is going quicker!" You cannot concentrate the same way you can in a private test.

'In private testing,' Emerson added, 'everybody is thinking about what they have to do to improve the car, not to go quicker. Not to do a quick time, but to improve the car. That's the big difference. You arrive at the track and you know that you can spend nearly all day just trying to get the car right – the ratios and wings and tyres. You stop at the pit and you talk to the team manager and the mechanics. You say the car is doing this and that. They have time to think before making a decision. That's the difference. Jackie Stewart is the one who started that, with tyre testing.'

In his Lotus years, Fittipaldi's ability to test and develop complemented Colin Chapman's fecundity of ideas. 'Somebody has to be thinking all the time, all during the year, about where you can improve,' the Brazilian said. 'You can never be happy and satisfied with the car and say, "Okay, now we did enough. Leave it alone for the next race." If you don't change it, you have to at least *try* to improve it. You have to see where you are losing, to improve it in the right way. That's what makes a Grand Prix car a winning car, a winning team. Everybody has to try to improve – the tyre people, the mechanics, the team manager, the designer, the driver. Because the competition is very hard.'

Emerson quickly gained credibility in the Lotus team for his technical knack. 'He remembers changes that he has made before,' said Lotus chief mechanic Eddie Dennis, 'and he'll dispute these with the "Old Man" and not just take something as gospel. He'll come back at him now and say: "We tried that before and I didn't like it like that" – which is very good. He certainly has a great sensitivity for the car – the same sort of feeling for it that Jimmy Clark had, if not more so. He saved a couple of engines by watching the gauges and just feeling a slight change in the power of the engine.'

For obvious reasons Fittipaldi felt a kinship with another driver who scored his first Formula 1 victory in a Lotus: his countryman Ayrton Senna. Jo Ramirez related a first encounter with this great talent at a Copersucar test at Silverstone. 'Emerson and I were sitting there talking when this young Brazilian came up, very shyly, to say hello to Emerson. After he left, Emerson said to me, "Watch this kid. He is going to be one of the greatest ever in the sport."'

The two champions came to know each other well. 'I've known him since he was 12 years old,' said Fittipaldi, 'and he really looked up to me. I think in the beginning he looked at me as his mentor. He was an incredible driver. As far as natural talent goes, he may have been the best ever.' His death at the wheel of a car 'was something that we never expected would happen to him. The world lost the greatest athlete in the history of motor racing, and I have lost a great friend. Grand Prix racing will never be the same without Ayrton.'

Just as a generation of Brazilians followed Emerson into Formula 1, so too did they exploit the trail he blazed into Indycar racing. One of the most successful, Helio Castroneves, also hailed from Sao Paulo and established his American base in Miami. Fittipaldi managed the career of Castroneves, who in 2002 became the first man to win the Indianapolis 500 two years running since Al Unser in 1971. Castroneves took no chances, wielding *two* bottles of milk and pouring them over his head before celebrating by climbing the chain-link fence. Emerson has also been a staunch cheering section for his nephew Christian's CART career.

Having embraced CART-style racing after Fittipaldi's involvement, Brazil continued to benefit from his initiatives. He was behind the conversion of the track near Rio into a high-speed circuit that staged a number of CART contests and he helped bring live coverage of CART races to Brazil. In the 21st Century he was still active in exploring new sites for a Brazilian CART round. One candidate was the beautiful city of Salvador, capital of the state of Bahia. Emerson and his team surveyed the city and recommended a possible road course that included the beach, Monaco-style.

Fittipaldi's other businesses in Brazil benefited from his availability in retirement. These included Fittipaldi Motor Accessories, offering a line of fashion and motoring items, a Mercedes-Benz dealership and a participation in the Brazilian arm of German fashion house Hugo Boss. His Boss connection led Emerson to open the first licensed Hugo Boss franchise in the US during his Miami

residence. Still in touch with Ralph Sanchez, he lent his support to the promoter's effort to bring sports-prototype racing back to the streets of Miami.

Anything but accident-prone during his racing career, Fittipaldi started catching up in retirement in the autumn of 1997 when he crashed his microlight aircraft near his country estate with his 6-year-old son Luca aboard. Fortunately Luca was fine, able to help ward off the vultures attracted by his father's blood until help arrived. He recovered well from his spinal and arm injuries. Further aerial adventures were curtailed when the authorities discovered that his flying licence had long expired. Then just before Christmas of 2001 Emerson suffered hand and collarbone fractures when his bicycle tripped over another in the darkness not far from his Miami home. He was patched up by the same doctors who repaired him after his Michigan speedway crash more than five years earlier.

Though no longer competing, Emerson Fittipaldi still loved driving. 'Driving a car on a track, quickly, by myself – I find pleasure in doing that,' he said. He gave a lot of pleasure to others in 1997 when he raced up Goodwood's hill in his Penske Indycar at the Festival of Speed. 'Some people like to play golf, some people like to play football. I like to drive, myself, alone. I really love cars. If I am on the road and a nice girl goes by, I have a look; it is like that with a beautiful car. If it is a very good one I can stay looking at it for about two hours.'

For the cars, the feeling was mutual. Few drivers treated them with such consummate care, intelligence and gentleness, while at the same time extracting every iota of their performance potential. If the Lotuses, McLarens, Fittipaldis, Marches, Lolas and Penskes could talk, they'd return the compliment. 'Thanks for the rides, Emerson,' they'd say. 'We did well together.'

When the Fittipaldi brothers become BMW car and motorcycle importers for Brazil the Munich company is understandably delighted. Their prominence in Brazilian sporting and business circles helps the brothers establish fruitful business ventures in their home country.

The charming and lovely Maria Helena Fittipaldi strongly supports her husband's career and masters the art of timing and scoring. However, their marriage doesn't survive the travails of the Copersucar era. In 1997 Emerson races a Penske-Mercedes up the hill at the Goodwood Festival and joins the author for a book launch. At Riverside in 1973 he three-wheels a Porsche Carrera in the IROC races.

In the IROC contests of 1974 (above) and 1975 (opposite) Emerson wheels heavy American metal in the shape of Chevrolet Camaros. He acquits himself well against star drivers from Grand Prix racing, CART and NASCAR.

The Fittipaldi family hideaway at Guaruja on the Atlantic coast near Sao Paulo numbers a paddle-tennis court among its amenities (preceding pages and surrounding). Complete with Copersucar T-shirt, Emerson includes tennis and a mock battle with Maria Helena in his November 1976 exercise regime. Son Jayson also takes to the court. If life cannot be beautiful in Brazil, where can it be?

Annotated bibliography

Ball, Adrian, *My Greatest Race – by twenty of the finest racing drivers of all time*, edited for the Jim Clark Foundation (E. P. Dutton, New York, NY, 1974). 139pp. 68 photographs.

Content exactly as the title suggests. Emerson chose his first race of the 1973 season, the Argentine Grand Prix, in which he felt himself to be under severe pressure as the reigning champion competing under the eyes of his South American compatriots. He defeated Messrs. Peterson, Ickx, Stewart, Cevert and Regazzoni to take the lead with 10 laps to go. 'I am proud to have won in such company,' said the modest Fittipaldi.

Crombac, Gerard 'Jabby' *Colin Chapman – The Man and His Cars* (Patrick Stephens Limited, Wellingborough, Northants, 1986). 383pp. 242 b/w photographs.

Magnum opus on Chapman by long-time friend and veteran French F1 writer Jabby Crombac which completely ignores the De Lorean scandal. The Foreword is by Enzo Ferrari, no less! Good perspectives and insights on the Fittipaldi years at Lotus, including the controversial issue of his pairing with Ronnie Peterson in 1973. Recently reprinted by Haynes.

Cutter, Robert and Fendell, Bob, *The Encyclopaedia of Auto Racing Greats* (Prentice-Hall Inc. Englewood Cliffs, NJ, 1973). 675pp. Hundreds of b/w photographs.

Vast pot pourri of racing biographies with Fittipaldi occupying more than two pages. This is a good book for those lesser-known individuals whom you keep reading about but wonder who they were. Inevitably many are American track racers. Understand-ably the American authors majored on Emerson's shock win at Watkins Glen in 1970. Their timing was just right to include his 1972 World Championship.

Fittipaldi, Emerson and Hayward, Elizabeth, *Flying on the Ground* (William Kimber, London, 1973). 256pp. 29 b/w photographs.

The value of this oddly named book lies in the actual identity of its co-author as Priscilla Phipps, who accompanied the Lotus team as timer and scorer with her husband David, ace photo-grapher. In this 'reader'-style work Emerson's early thoughts about the art and science of motor racing are well portrayed, as is his grisly road accident with Maria Helena in France in 1971.

Heglar, Mary Schnall, *The Grand Prix Champions* (Bond Parkhurst Books, Newport Beach, CA. 1973). 234pp. 102 photographs.

Centred on the period 1950–1972 and, as with other American books, giving a better insight into the human emotions of the subjects. Plenty of rarely-seen pictures. Fittipaldi was Heglar's newest champion and she researched him well, with many interesting quotes and insights. Best of all she captured his remarkable balance and unchanging character, calling him 'a delightful man'.

Henry, Alan, *Driving Forces – Fifty men who shaped the world of motor racing* (Patrick Stephens Limited, Sparkford, Somerset, 1992). 200pp. 74 b/w photographs.

As its title suggests, a brief look at the lives of various motorsport icons, drivers, constructors, entrants, team managers, officials, designers, engine builders etc. Each is given a neat if necessarily superficial write-up in the typical Henry style. Fittipaldi earns a place as a 'driving force' in a three-page writeup.

Hungness, Carl, *Indianapolis 500 Yearbook, 1986–1995* (Carl Hungness Publishing, 1986–1995). 223-240pp. Heavily illustrated with both colour and b/w photos.

Carl Hungness took over from American publishing pioneer and enthusiast Floyd Clymer as the editor and publisher of an annual yearbook about the Indianapolis 500-mile race. Each contains a rich mixture of material with a blow-by-blow account of qualifying – often the most interesting part of the event – and the race, plus interviews and profiles of key players. Although light on technical insights, an essential record of each race.

Kirby, Gordon, *Emerson Fittipaldi* (Hazleton Publishing, Richmond, Surrey, 1990). 107pp. 86 b/w photographs, 20 in colour.

No one observes the CART and Indycar scene more astutely than Gordon Kirby or writes more authoritatively about it. Thus his large-format book about Fittipaldi is deepest in dealing with his American career but also covers his early years as well. Although not heavy on text, the book provides useful insights. Kirby has also collaborated with Emerson in a book titled *The Art of Motor Racing*.

Kirby, Gordon, 'Still Racy after All These Years' (*Racer*, September 1993). pp. 32–35, 7 colour photographs.

Kirby affectionately profiled the 'still racy' Brazilian at the age of 46 in the year in which he won the Indianapolis 500-mile race for the second time and kept interloper Nigel Mansell honest. Fitness in mind and body was key to the great driver's continued success, said Kirby.

Laban, Brian, editor, *Winners – A Who's Who of Motor Racing Champions* (Orbis Publishing, London, 1981). 190pp. 30 b/w photographs.

Concisely presented biographies of 123 racing drivers were compiled by Laban in this dense and useful volume. The section on Emerson was written by Mike Twite, whose views of his career are especially perceptive and insightful. It ends with Fittipaldi's retirement from the Grand Prix world.

Ludvigsen, Karl, 'Brazil's Grand Prix Challenger,' 'How I Rate the Formula 1 Cars,' 'How I Won the World Driving Championship' and 'The Bug That Roared.' *Various periodicals* (1973–1977).

During his visits and conversations with the Fittipaldis in this period, the author conducted interviews that resulted in four articles that were widely published at the time. Both Emerson and the author were contributors to the leading Brazilian car magazine *Quatro Rodas*.

Nye, Doug, *Great Racing Drivers* (Hamlyn Publishing Group, London, 1977). 156pp. Hundreds of b/w and colour photographs.

A superior pot-boiler from Doug Nye which covers the years between 1900 and 1976 and some of the drivers who excelled during that time. The text is limited and each subject including Fittipaldi is given a brief potted history, but there are plenty of pictures to compensate. It naturally ends in downbeat style, calling Emerson 'the two-time Champion who lost his way.'

Nye, Doug, *Lotus – '61–'71: Design Revolution* (Robert Bentley, Cambridge, MA. 1972). 288pp. Numerous b/w photographs.

The result of prodigious research by the indefatigable and well-informed Nye, this book has racing as its main theme with the Lotus production cars as variations. It has been invaluable in tracing the cars and events that saw Emerson Fittipaldi burst onto the European scene as the 'amazing Brazilian coffee bean'.

Nye, Doug, *McLaren: The Grand Prix, CanAm and Indycars* (Hazleton Publishing, Richmond, Surrey, 1984). 270pp. 100+ b/w photographs and a few in colour.

In the engaging Nye style this is a heady blend of personal testimony and race reporting with useful technical details, and all the more valuable for that. It is an important source for views on the McLaren effort during Fittipaldi's two years with them, a hugely competitive era in GP racing. It concludes just as the TAG turbo era is beginning; an update, please, Doug! And next time please add an index.

Pritchard, Anthony, *The World Champions – Guiseppe Farina to Jackie Stewart* (Macmillan Publishing, London, 1972). 253pp. 41 photographs.

This work by the diligent Pritchard covers all the World Champions up to and including 1972, thus ending with Our Hero. He is awarded 10 pages in a biography titled 'The Black Prince', a nickname awarded him by the *Daily Express* in recognition of his black JPS-Lotus racing cars. Noteworthy, as Pritchard says, were the simultaneous Formula 1 careers of two brothers, then unprecedented in the post-1950 era.

Rosberg, Keke and Botsford, Keith, *Keke* (Stanley Paul, London, 1985). 191pp. 26 b/w photographs.

In portmanteau format, both Rosberg and Botsford (in italics) have their say. Keke's contributions include excerpts from contemporary letters to his father. Rosberg is as feisty and up-front in words as in driving. 'There is no sport like F1 for frustration,' he says. 'There are moments of joy, but 75 per cent of the time there is frustration.' He minces no words about the frustrations of his two Fittipaldi seasons. Because many of his remarks ended up on the cutting-room floor, the reader is invited to assess Keke for himself.

Sakkis, Tony, *Indy Racing Legends* (Motorbooks International, Osceola, WI, 1996). 160pp. 184 b/w photographs.

With an easy style and ample black and white illustrations, Sakkis profiles 32 greats of the Indianapolis 500-mile race arranged alphabetically from Andretti to Unser. In between are the well-known, such as Eddie Rickenbacker and A.J. Foyt, and lesser-known heroes of the race like Jim McGee, Pat Patrick and Leo Goossen. Two-time-winner Emerson gets good coverage over five pages.

Sheldon, Paul, and Rabagliati, Duncan, *A Record of Grand Prix and Voiturette Racing*, Volumes 8, 9 and 10 (Shipley, 1994, 1995, 1996).

Although not complete in all respects (race numbers are sometimes missing) these meticulously prepared volumes are essential for any historian writing about motor racing. There are no illustrations but Paul Sheldon's text is often vivid as well as economical. They helped establish that Emerson's Copersucar years were not quite so disastrous as these have often been portrayed. They also provided essential insights into Fittipaldi's Formula 2 racing.

Small, Steve, *Grand Prix Who's Who – From Abecassis to Zunino* (Travel Publishing Ltd, 3rd Edition, Reading, 2000). 624pp. Hundreds of b/w portraits, some from the Ludvigsen Library.

A detailed reference work on every Grand Prix driver and the cars they drove from the inception of the F1 World Championship in 1950 to date of publication. With the help of his friends, Small has made this the standard work on the subject, vastly expanding it in this Third Edition. Emerson is on pages 203–206 and brother Wilson is on pages 207–208.

Tommasi, Tommasso, *Emerson Fittipaldi* (L'Editrice dell'Automobile, Milan, 1973). 112pp. Richly illustrated with poster enclosure.

In landscape format, this softbound book is a warm tribute to a new World Champion whose Italian origins meant that he was taken to Italy's heart. In Italian, it has numerous early quotes of interest and value about Emerson's career.

Williams, Geoffrey, *McLaren – A Racing History* (Crowood Press, Marlborough, Wilts, 1991). 333pp. 100+ colour and b/w photographs.

Though many photos are disappointing, this history through the 1990 season is of value, with sidebars on drivers and other key personalities. Especially useful are tables of chassis numbers and practice times for all championship F1 entries. It provides good detail on the development and exploits of the M23, Emerson's 1974 championship chariot.

In addition to these specific citations the pages of many contemporary periodicals and annuals have contributed to this telling of the Fittipaldi story. Among them are *The Motor*, *The Autocar*, *Quatro Rodas*, *Autosport*, *Autoweek*, *Autocourse*, *Road & Track*, *Car and Driver*, *Racer*, *On Track* and *Competition Press*. These have been accessed in the Ludvigsen Library.

Frequent reference has been made to the excellent website www.forix.com, which provides outstanding historical statistics on all aspects of Formula 1 racing. Helpful as well were the Indianapolis Motor Speedway's website, my.brickyard.com, and http://www.irocracing.com, the website of the IROC series. Comments in The Nostalgia Forum of Atlas F1 at http://www.atlasf1.com have also been of interest and value.

Photograph credits

Max Le Grand from Ludvigsen Library: front end paper, P45 upper, P48, PP66–67, P68, P69, P100, P101, P106.

Karl Ludvigsen from Ludvigsen Library: P24, P32, P33, P35 upper, P45 lower, PP46–47, P55, P56, P57, P60, P61, P65, P70, P71, PP72-73, P98, P99 upper left, P102 middle, P138, P139, P194 left, P198, P199, P200, P201.

Ludvigsen Library: P2, P31, P34 upper, P34 lower, P36, P43, P44, PP58–59, PP62–63, P64, P75, P76, P80, P88, P89, PP90–91, PP94–95, P103 lower, P193, P194 right.

Ove Nielsen from Ludvigsen Library: P9, P74, P77, PP78–79, P87, P92, P93, P96, P97, P99, P102 upper, P102 lower, P108, P109, P112, P113, P114, P115, P116, P117, PP118–119, P120, P121, P122, P123, PP124–125, P126, P127, PP128–129, P130, P137, P140, P141 lower, P142 lower, PP144–145, P146, P147, P148, P149, PP150–151, P152, P153, P156, P157, PP158-159, back end paper.

Bob Tronolone: P10, P17, P18, P19, PP20–21, PP22–23, P103 upper, P103 middle, PP104–105, P107, P110, P111, P141 upper, P142 upper, P143, PP154–155, P160, P167, P168, P169, PP170-171, P172, P173, PP174–175, P176, P177, PP178–179, P180, P181, PP182–183, P184, P185, P186, P195, P196, P197.

Index